HUANGGANG XIAO ZHUANGYUAN ZUOYEBEN

四年级英语下 RP
SI NIANJI YINGYU XIA

主　　编　万志勇
本册主编　代　欣　程　颖　张婷婷　周文华　张文涛
　　　　　舒红艳　范丽萍　叶慧宏　赵　晶

龍門書局
北京

目录

Unit 1　My school

A. Let's talk　Look, ask and answer …………………………… 1

A. Let's learn　Let's do ………… 2

A. Let's spell …………………… 4

◎ Unit 1　阶段复习 …………… 5

B. Let's talk　Let's play ………… 8

B. Let's learn　Look, ask and answer ………………………… 9

B. Read and write-Let's sing …… 11

C. Story time …………………… 13

◎ Unit 1　听力训练 …………… 14

Unit 2　What time is it?

A. Let's talk　Let's play ……… 15

A. Let's learn　Let's do ……… 16

A. Let's spell ………………… 18

◎ Unit 2　阶段复习 ………… 19

B. Let's talk　Let's play ……… 22

B. Let's learn　Let's play …… 23

B. Read and write-Let's sing … 25

C. Story time ………………… 27

◎ Unit 2　听力训练 ………… 28

Unit 3　Weather

A. Let's talk　Let's play ……… 29

A. Let's learn　Let's chant …… 30

A. Let's spell ………………… 32

◎ Unit 3　阶段复习 ………… 33

B. Let's talk　Let's play ……… 36

B. Let's learn　Let's play …… 37

B. Read and write-Let's sing … 39

C. Story time ………………… 41

◎ Unit 3　听力训练 ………… 42

Unit 4   At the farm

- A. Let's talk   Let's play ········ 43
- A. Let's learn   Let's chant ······ 44
- A. Let's spell ···················· 46
- ◎ Unit 4   阶段复习 ············· 47
- B. Let's talk   Let's play ········ 50
- B. Let's learn   Draw and say ··· 51
- B. Read and write-Let's sing ······ 53
- C. Story time ···················· 55
- ◎ Unit 4   听力训练 ············· 56

Unit 5   My clothes

- A. Let's talk   Let's play ········ 57
- A. Let's learn   Let's do ········ 58
- A. Let's spell ···················· 60
- ◎ Unit 5   阶段复习 ············· 61
- B. Let's talk   Let's find out ··· 64
- B. Let's learn   Let's find out ··· 65
- B. Read and write-Let's sing ······ 67

- C. Story time ···················· 69
- ◎ Unit 5   听力训练 ············· 70

Unit 6   Shopping

- A. Let's talk   Let's play ········ 71
- A. Let's learn   Complete and say ··········· 72
- A. Let's spell ···················· 74
- ◎ Unit 6   阶段复习 ············· 75
- B. Let's talk   Let's act ········ 78
- B. Let's learn   Let's play ······ 79
- B. Read and write-Let's sing ··· 81
- C. Story time ···················· 83
- ◎ Unit 6   听力训练 ············· 84

附 录

Ⅰ 册 知识清单

Ⅱ 卷 核心能力评价 + 听力材料及参考答案

Unit 1 My school

A. Let's talk Look, ask and answer

夯实基础

一、选择正确的答案,将其序号填入题前括号里。

(   )1. Excuse _____. Where's Classroom 2?

    A. I   B. my   C. me

(   )2. The teachers' office is _____ to the library.

    A. near   B. next to   C. next

(   )3. _____ my homework.

    A. Here is   B. Here are   C. Here

二、学校来了一位新同学,他正在向 Sarah 询问学校的情况。根据图片选择正确的答案,在相应的括号里打"√"。

Excuse me. Where is the teachers' office?

1. (   ) A. It's on the second floor.
   (   ) B. It's next to Classroom 1.
   (   ) C. It's next to the library.

Is it next to Classroom 2?

2. (   ) A. It's next to Classroom 3.
   (   ) B. Yes, it is.
   (   ) C. No, it isn't.

三、看图,判断下列对话与图片是否相符,相符的写"T",不相符的写"F"。

(   )1. —Is this the teachers' office?

    —No, it isn't. This is my classroom.

(   )2. —Where's the library?
—It's on the second floor.

(   )3. —Where's Classroom 1?
—It's next to Classroom 3.

Library
Teachers' Office

Classroom 2	
Classroom 3	Classroom 1

提升能力

四、观察图片，从方框中选择合适的单词或短语写在横线上。

on   next to   teachers' office   second floor

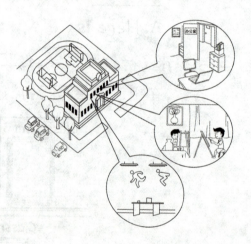

Dear Windy,

　　How are you? This is my new school in China. The school is great. An art room with a beautiful picture is 1._____ the 2._____. A 3._____ and a gym are 4._____ it. Of course, a big playground is in my school, too.

　　　　　　　　　　　　　　　　Love,
　　　　　　　　　　　　　　　　James

A. Let's learn　Let's do

夯实基础

一、选择正确的单词或短语补全句子。

1. _____(When/Where) is our classroom?
2. The teachers' office is on the _____(first/one) floor.
3. There are _____(second/two) floors in the building(建筑物).
4. Go to the _____(teachers' office/playground). Have a PE class.
5. Go to the _____(garden/library). Find a book.

二、看图,选择合适的句子,将其序号填在图片下的括号里。

1. (   )   2. (   )   3. (   )   4. (   )

A. Go to the garden. Water the flowers.
B. Go to the library. Read a book.
C. Go to the playground. Play football.
D. Go to the teachers' office. Say hello.

三、选择合适的句子补全对话,将其序号填在横线上。

Jim: Mike, you have a big and nice school! 1. _____

Mike: It's on the first floor.

Jim: Where is the library?

Mike: 2. _____

Jim: 3. _____

Mike: Good idea!

Jim: 4. _____

Mike: Great! I like storybooks very much.

A. We can read storybooks in the library.
B. Where's your classroom?
C. Let's go to the library.
D. It's on the second floor.

提升能力

四、根据龙一鸣的描述,选择正确的图片,将其序号写在横线上。

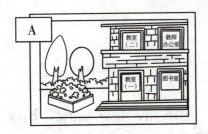 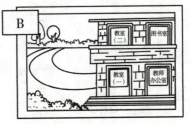 

My school is _____. — Long Yiming

My school is nice. Classroom 1 is on the first floor. The teachers' office is next to it. Classroom 2 and the library are on the second floor. I'm in Classroom 2 and I often read books in the library. We also have a big playground. I often play football there. Welcome to my school.

A. Let's spell

夯实基础

一、听录音,根据图片补全单词,完成小韵文。

Jennif_e_ r is having din_ _ _

with h_ _ sis_ _ _, Jane.

Jennifer says, "Let's eat all the vegetables.

I will be bet_ _ _.

I will be a shoo_ _ _(射击运动员)."

"Yes. But I will be a ba_ _ _," Jane says.

二、读句子,圈出每个句子中含有与例词画线部分相同发音的单词。

1. His sist<u>er</u> is a driver. She likes winter.

2. His moth<u>er</u> is a dancer. She is playing computer games.

3. This tig<u>er</u> isn't a good runner, but it's a good swimmer.

提升能力

三、看图,完成下面的句子。

1. My _____ is ready.

2. Look! I have a pencil, an _____ and a _____ in my new pencil box.

3. I _____ the flowers in the garden with my little _____.

Unit 1 阶段复习

听力部分

一、听录音,选择你所听到的单词或短语,将其序号填入题前括号里。

( )1. A. water B. winter

( )2. A. under B. number

( )3. A. first B. second

( )4. A. playground B. library

( )5. A. teachers' office B. teacher's desk

二、听录音,用数字给下列图片排序。

( ) ( ) ( ) ( ) ( )

三、听录音,判断下列图片与你所听到的内容是否相符,相符的在括号里打"√",不相符的打"×"。

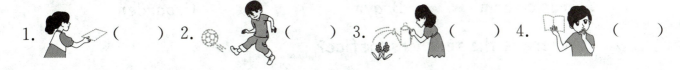

1. ( ) 2. ( ) 3. ( ) 4. ( )

四、听对话,选择正确的答案,将其序号填入题前括号里。

听第一段对话,完成第1、2小题。

( )1. The girl's school is _____.
    A. big   B. beautiful   C. small

( )2. The playground is next to the _____.
    A. library   B. gym   C. garden

听第二段对话，完成第3、4小题。

( )3. The library is on the _____ floor.
　　A. first　　　　B. second　　　　C. third

( )4. The teachers' office is next to _____.
　　A. Classroom 1　　B. Classroom 3　　C. the library

读写部分

五、选择每组单词中不同类的一项，将其序号填入题前括号里。

( )1. A. library　　　　B. gym　　　　　C. bedroom
( )2. A. first　　　　　B. two　　　　　C. second
( )3. A. play　　　　　B. read　　　　　C. storybook
( )4. A. school　　　　B. teacher　　　　C. student
( )5. A. flower　　　　B. beautiful　　　C. big

六、选择正确的答案，将其序号填入题前括号里。

( )1. Go to the playground. Play _____ football.
　　A. the　　　　　　B. /　　　　　　C. a

( )2. Water the flowers in the _____.
　　A. music room　　B. gym　　　　　C. garden

( )3. —Where is the teachers' office?
　　—_____
　　A. It's on the first floor.
　　B. Yes, it is.
　　C. This is the teachers' office.

( )4. Go to the _____. Read a book.
　　A. library　　　　B. bathroom　　　C. kitchen

七、选择合适的单词或短语补全对话,将其序号填在横线上。

A. welcome   B. second   C. No
D. Excuse   E. Thank you   F. Classroom 2

1. Amy: _____ me. Where is Classroom 4?
   Mike: It's on the _____ floor.
   Amy: _____.

2. Amy: Hello, Sarah. Is this Classroom 4?
   Sarah: _____, it isn't. This is _____. Classroom 4 is next to Classroom 5.
   Amy: OK. Thanks.
   Sarah: You're _____.

八、看图,补全下面的短文。

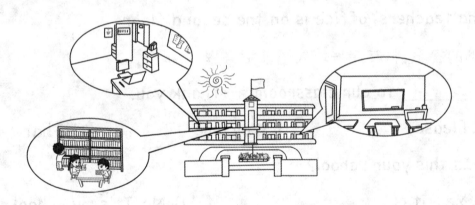

Welcome to our 1. _____. It's very big. Look! There are many books in the 2. _____. It is on the second floor. It's my favourite place (最喜欢的地方). The 3. _____ is on the second floor too. It is nice and clean. Is this my classroom? No, it isn't. My classroom is on the 4. _____. After class, we can play football on the 5. _____. It's fun.

B. Let's talk Let's play

夯实基础

一、为下列句子选择合适的图片，将其序号填入题前括号里。

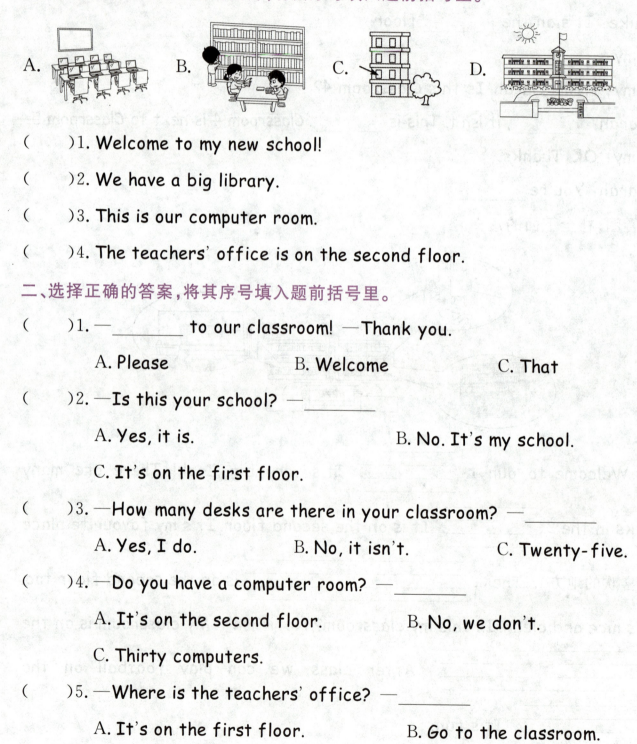

(　　)1. Welcome to my new school!

(　　)2. We have a big library.

(　　)3. This is our computer room.

(　　)4. The teachers' office is on the second floor.

二、选择正确的答案，将其序号填入题前括号里。

(　　)1. —_____ to our classroom! —Thank you.

　　A. Please　　　　B. Welcome　　　　C. That

(　　)2. —Is this your school? —_____

　　A. Yes, it is.　　　　　　　B. No. It's my school.

　　C. It's on the first floor.

(　　)3. —How many desks are there in your classroom? —_____

　　A. Yes, I do.　　　B. No, it isn't.　　　C. Twenty-five.

(　　)4. —Do you have a computer room? —_____

　　A. It's on the second floor.　　　B. No, we don't.

　　C. Thirty computers.

(　　)5. —Where is the teachers' office? —_____

　　A. It's on the first floor.　　　B. Go to the classroom.

　　C. Thank you.

Unit 1

🌐 提升能力

三、下图是学校某栋教学楼。假设有记者来到你的学校采访,请你根据图中信息回答记者的问题。

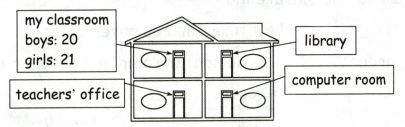

1. How many students are there in your class?

_____

2. Where is your classroom?

_____

3. Do you have a library?

_____

4. Look at the room under your classroom. Is that the computer room?

_____

◆ B. Let's learn   Look, ask and answer ◆

夯实基础

一、看图,选择合适的单词或短语补全句子,将其序号填在横线上。

A. music room   B. playground   C. art room   D. computer room

1.

We have computer classes in the _____.

2.

We draw pictures in the _____.

3.

We sing and dance in the _____.

4.

We play football on the _____.

二、选择正确的答案,将其序号填入题前括号里。

( )1. —_____ —Yes, we do.
　　A. Do you have a playground?　　B. Is this your playground?
　　C. Where is the playground?

( )2. Go to the _____. It's time for computer class.
　　A. playground　　B. computer room　　C. music room

( )3. We have _____ art room.
　　A. an　　B. a　　C. /

( )4. —This is my school. —_____
　　A. Thank you.　　B. Cool!　　C. You're welcome.

三、判断下列句子或对话与图片是否相符,相符的在括号里打"√",不相符的打"×"。

( )1. The computer room is on the second floor.

( )2. —Where is the classroom?
　　—It's on the second floor and next to the art room.

( )3. —Is that the garden?
　　—Yes, it is.

music room	
computer room	

art room	classroom
teachers' office	library

提升能力

四、按要求完成下列各题。

1. —Do you have a music room?（看图回答问题）
—_____, _____.

2. The library is on the _____ floor.（看图补全句子）

3. room, computer, Is, the, that （?）（连词成句）
_____

10

B. Read and write-Let's sing

夯实基础

一、根据对话内容，在图中空白处填入相应房间的英文名称。

Library			Art Room
Classroom 1		Teachers' Office	

—Do you have a computer room?

—Yes. It's on the second floor.

—Do you have a music room?

—Yes. It's next to Classroom 1.

—Where is the gym?

—It's under the art room.

—Where's Classroom 2?

—It's on the second floor. It's next to the art room.

二、看图补全句子，并进行仿写。

1. This is the _____.

2.  That is the _____.

3. _____

4.  _____

提升能力

三、读绘本故事,完成下列任务。

1

The tiger wants to eat the rooster.

2

The tiger dresses up as a rooster singer. The 1._____ dresses up as a rooster 2._____.

3

But the 3._____ knows it is the tiger.

4

Wow! A beautiful 4._____. The rooster loves it.

5

He runs to it. But he knows it is a danger(危险).

6

What can the rooster do? Then what's wrong with the tiger?

任务一:找出文中含有字母组合 er 且该组合发音相同的单词,将其写在方框中的横线上。(相同单词不重复写)

| danger   dancer   flower   _____   _____   _____ |

任务二:从上面的方框中选择合适的单词补全故事。

任务三:故事的最后"What can the rooster do?",有以下两种解决方案,你会选择哪一种呢?请在句末的括号里打"√",并和同伴说说你的理由。

Plan A: The rooster dresses up as a farmer with a hammer(锤子). (   )

Plan B: The rooster asks a farmer for help. (   )

C. Story time

一、选择正确的答案,将其序号填入题前括号里。

( ) 1. —Welcome to our school. This way, please.
　　—_____ beautiful!
　　A. What　　　　B. How　　　　C. Where

( ) 2. It's time _____ lunch.
　　A. for　　　　B. to　　　　C. on

( ) 3. 你想知道那是不是音乐教室,你可以问:
　　A. Is that the lunch room?　　B. Is this the art room?
　　C. Is that the music room?

( ) 4. 你吃饱了,你可以说:
　　A. I'm OK.　　B. I'm full.　　C. I'm sorry.

二、阅读短文,完成下列各题。

　　Hello, I'm Susan. Welcome to my school. Look! We have a gym, a canteen and a library. We can play sports, eat lunch and read books on the first floor. There is a music room, an art room and a dormitory on the second floor. We can sing songs, draw pictures and sleep in these rooms. We also have other(其他的) twenty-four rooms in our school. I love my school.

1. —How many rooms are there in Susan's school? —_____
　　A. 6.　　　　B. 13.　　　　C. 30.

2. Susan can eat lunch in the _____. She can sleep in the _____.

　　A　　B　　C　　D　　E　　F

3. Can you tell us some rooms in your school?

_____

_____

Unit 1 听力训练

一、听录音,选择你所听到的单词,将其序号填入题前括号里。

( ) 1. A. water   B. tiger   C. sister

( ) 2. A. dinner   B. ruler   C. computer

( ) 3. A. under   B. number   C. eraser

( ) 4. A. winter   B. after   C. river

( ) 5. A. teacher   B. keeper   C. writer

二、听录音,用数字给下列图片排序。

 ( )  ( )  ( )

 ( ) 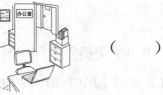 ( )  ( )

三、听录音,选择正确的答语,将其序号填入题前括号里。

( ) 1. A. It's on the first floor.   B. I like it.   C. It is big.

( ) 2. A. Yes. It's a gym.   B. No, it isn't.   C. It's a library.

( ) 3. A. Thirty-one.   B. It's on the second floor.
       C. This way, please.

( ) 4. A. Yes, it is.   B. Yes, we do.   C. Yes, we don't.

四、听对话,判断下列句子正误,正确的写"T",错误的写"F"。

( ) 1. The library is on the first floor in Amy's school.

( ) 2. The students often read books in the library.

( ) 3. The teachers' room is next to the art room.

( ) 4. Chen Jie can sing and dance in the music room.

Unit 2 What time is it?

A. Let's talk Let's play

夯实基础

一、选择正确的单词或短语补全句子。

1. School is _____ (after/over/on).

2. Time _____ (is/to/for) go to school.

3. Let's _____ (go/go to/to go) home.

4. It's time _____ (of/for/have) lunch.

二、判断下列句子与图中时间是否相符,相符的在括号里打"√",不相符的打"×"。

1. It's seven o'clock.   (   )

2. It's twelve o'clock.   (   )

3. It's 6:00.   (   )

4. It's 1:05.   (   )

5. It's five fifty.   (   )

6. It's 6:30.   (   )

三、请根据小朋友们的描述,选择相应的时间,将其序号填在括号里。

1. I'm Fangfang. I'm in New York. It's 7:10 a.m. now.   (   )

2. I'm Mingming. I'm in Beijing. It's 8:10 p.m. now.   (   )

3. I'm Dingding. I'm in Sydney. It's 10:10 p.m. now.   (   )

4. I'm Bingbing. I'm in London. It's 12:10 p.m. now.   (   )

A.   B.   C.   D.

提升能力

四、Lingling 正在与好朋友 Malina 和 Lucas 在微信上聊天。Malina 和 Lucas 分别来自 Seattle 和 London，请你根据世界时钟上的时间和对话内容，补全对话。

Lingling: In Beijing, it's 1._____. What 2._____ is it in Seattle, Malina?

Malina: It's 3._____. It's time for 4._____. Good night, Lingling.

Lingling: Good night. What about you, Lucas?

Lucas: It's 5._____ in London. It's time to 6._____. See you, Lingling.

World Clock

Today, +0HRS Beijing — 14:30
Today, −16HRS Seattle — 22:30
Today, −8HRS London — 6:30

A. Let's learn Let's do

夯实基础

一、仿照例子，将对应的图文连线。

1. It's twelve o'clock.   A.   a. PE class
2. It's five o'clock.   B.   b. dinner
3. It's ten o'clock.   C.   c. lunch
4. It's two o'clock.   D.   d. English class
5. It's three o'clock.   E.   e. music class

二、选择合适的单词补全句子,将其序号填入题前括号里。(每项限选一次)

A. Chinese   B. music   C. art   D. maths   E. English   F. PE

(   )1. We learn ABC Song in _____ class.

(   )2. We play sports in _____ class.

(   )3. We count numbers in _____ class.

(   )4. We sing and dance in _____ class.

(   )5. We draw pictures in _____ class.

(   )6. We read Thoughts on a Tranquil Night(《静夜思》) in _____ class.

三、判断下列句子与图片是否相符,相符的在括号里写"T",不相符的写"F"。

(   )1. It's time for PE class.

(   )2. It's time for art class.

(   )3. It's time for breakfast.

提升能力

四、按要求完成下列各题。

1. —What time is it?（看图回答问题）
   —_____

2. Let's _____ and _____. （看图补全句子）

3. Time for _____. （看图补全句子）

4. time, English, It's, for, class   (.)（连词成句）
   _____

5. some, eat, Let's, rice   (.)（连词成句）
   _____

A. Let's spell

夯实基础

一、听录音,根据图片补全单词,完成歌谣。

Little b__d, little b____, what do you see?

I see a green t____tle looking at me.

Green t__t__, green _____, what do you see?

I see a p____ple fish looking at me.

P__p__ fish, _____ fish, what do you see?

I see a nice g____l looking at me.

注意 ir 和 ur 的发音规律哟!

二、判断每组单词画线部分的读音是否相同,相同的打"√",不相同的打"×"。

( ) 1. A. b<u>ir</u>d   B. b<u>ir</u>th   C. hamb<u>ur</u>ger

( ) 2. A. h<u>ur</u>t   B. b<u>ur</u>n   C. sh<u>ir</u>t

( ) 3. A. sh<u>or</u>t   B. p<u>ur</u>se   C. n<u>ur</u>se

( ) 4. A. g<u>ir</u>l   B. dinn<u>er</u>   C. numb<u>er</u>

提升能力

三、看图,选择正确的单词完成句子。

1. The boy has a _____ for _____ .

2. My _____ is a _____ .

3. This little _____ likes the _____ .

nurse
girl
hamburger
bird
sister
dinner

Unit 2 阶段复习

听力部分

一、听录音,选择你所听到的单词或短语,将其序号填入题前括号里。

( )1. A. dirt　　　　　　　　B. birth

( )2. A. hamburger　　　　　B. number

( )3. A. thirty　　　　　　　B. thirteen

( )4. A. lunch　　　　　　　B. dinner

( )5. A. PE class　　　　　　B. music class

二、听录音,选择与你所听到的内容相符的图片,将其序号填入题前括号里。

( )1. It's 9:00. It's time for _____.

 A.　　 B.　　 C.

( )2. It's 7:00. It's time for _____.

 A.　　 B.　　 C.

( )3. Let's _____.

 A.　　 B.　　 C.

三、听录音,选择正确的答语,将其序号填入题前括号里。

( )1. A. Let's go to the playground.　　B. Let's go to the music room.

( )2. A. It's time for maths class.　　　B. It's 10 o'clock.

( )3. A. It's on the first floor.　　　　　B. It's big.

( )4. A. Let's eat some rice.　　　　　B. Let's sing and dance.

四、听对话,判断下列句子正误,正确的写"T",错误的写"F"。

(   )1. Tom is in Sydney.

(   )2. It's 9 o'clock in Sydney now.

(   )3. It's 10 o'clock in Beijing now.

(   )4. It's time for lunch in Beijing.

(   )5. It's time for English class in Sydney.

读写部分

五、选择每组单词中不同类的一项,将其序号填入题前括号里。

(   )1. A. lunch   B. dinner   C. time

(   )2. A. China   B. London   C. Sydney

(   )3. A. first   B. ten   C. twelve

(   )4. A. jump   B. drink   C. milk

(   )5. A. PE   B. class   C. music

六、为下列图片选择合适的句子,将其序号填入题前括号里。

(   )1.

A. Let's go to the playground.

B. Let's go to the art room.

(   )2.

A. It's time for Chinese class.

B. It's time for English class.

(   )3.

A. We can jump and run in PE class.

B. We can sing and dance in music class.

(   )4.

A. A nurse and her hamburger.

B. A girl and her bird.

七、选择正确的答案,将其序号填入题前括号里。

(   )1. I _____ breakfast at 7 o'clock.

A. is   B. has   C. have

(　)2. It's 2 o'clock. It's time _____ PE class.
　　A. in　　　　　　B. for　　　　　　C. to

(　)3. It's time _____ watch TV.
　　A. to　　　　　　B. for　　　　　　C. at

(　)4. It's _____ o'clock.
　　A. six　　　　　B. 6:00　　　　　C. eight five

(　)5. I'm _____ London. It's 12:10 p.m.
　　A. on　　　　　B. to　　　　　　C. in

八、给下列句子选择合适的答语, 将其序号填入题前括号里。

(　)1. What time is it, John?
(　)2. Let's go to the playground.
(　)3. Where are you, Sarah?
(　)4. It's 6 p.m. Time for dinner!

A. I'm in New York.
B. It's 10 o'clock. It's time for bed.
C. Oh! Let's go home together.
D. OK. Let's go.

九、任务型阅读。

Time	7 a.m.	9 a.m.	12 p.m.	2 p.m.	3 p.m.	6 p.m.
Activity	breakfast	English class	lunch	music class	PE class	dinner

任务一: 将时间和对应的活动连线。

1.　　　　2.　　　　3.　　　　4.

A.　　　　B.　　　　C.　　　　D.

任务二: 根据表格内容完成下列句子。

1. It's six o'clock in the evening. It's time for _____.
2. It's seven o'clock in the morning. _____.
3. It's twelve o'clock. _____.

B. Let's talk Let's play

夯实基础

一、根据对话内容选择正确的答案,在相应的方框里打"√"。

1. Jack: What time is it?
   Mum: It's 6 o'clock. It's time to eat dinner.
   Jack: OK!

   ☐ A. 9 a.m.   ☐ B. 6 a.m.   ☐ C. 6 p.m.

2. Teacher: Boys and girls, it's time for art class.
   Students: We are ready!

   ☐ A.   ☐ B.   ☐ C.

3. Mum: Hurry up!
   ☐ A. It's time to eat lunch.
   ☐ B. It's time to get up.
   ☐ C. It's time to go to the playground.
   Sam: OK!

二、选择正确的答案,将其序号填入题前括号里。

(　　) 1. It's two _____.
  A. o'clock　　B. clock　　C. clocks

(　　) 2. —What time is it now? —_____
  A. It's 8 yuan.　　B. It's black.　　C. It's 1:00.

(　　) 3. Dinner is _____.
  A. ready　　B. read　　C. really

22

( )4. It's time _____ go to bed.
   A. to   B. for   C. at

( )5. It's time _____ maths class.
   A. at   B. to   C. for

提升能力

三、看图，完成下面的句子。

1. It's _____ o'clock. It's time for _____.
2. It's _____ o'clock. It's time for _____ class.
3. It's _____ o'clock. It's time for _____.
4. It's _____ o'clock. It's time for _____ class.
5. It's _____ o'clock. It's time for _____ class.
6. It's _____ o'clock. It's time for _____ class.

B. Let's learn Let's play

夯实基础

一、看图，为下列图片选择相应的短语，将其序号填入相应的括号里。

A. go home   B. go to school   C. go to bed   D. get up

1. ( ) 2. ( ) 3. ( ) 4. ( )

二、选择合适的单词补全句子。

1. It's 6:30. It's time _____ get up.
2. It's 9:20. It's time _____ Chinese class.
3. It's 5:30. It's time _____ dinner.
4. It's 10:40. It's time _____ have an English class.

三、判断下列句子与图片是否相符,相符的在括号里打"√",不相符的打"×"。

(　　)1. It's 6:00. I get up.　　(　　)2. I do my homework at 8:00.
(　　)3. She goes to bed at 9:00.　(　　)4. He goes to school at 7:00.

提升能力

四、任务型阅读。

　　Hi, I'm Mike. Usually I get up at six thirty. Then I have breakfast at seven o'clock. I often go to school at seven thirty. Class begins at eight o'clock. I have lunch at school at twelve o'clock. School is over at four o'clock in the afternoon. Then I go home at four thirty. I have dinner at six o'clock. And I go to bed at nine o'clock. This is my day. I'm very busy.

任务一:根据短文内容,完成下面的表格。

get up		have lunch		
	7:30		4:30	9:00

任务二:选择正确的答案,将其序号填入题前括号里。

(　　)1. Class starts at _____.
　　A. 7:30　　　B. 8:00　　　C. 8:30

(　　)2. Mike has lunch _____.
　　A. at home　　B. in a restaurant　　C. at school

任务三:仿照画线句子,写一写你的日常生活。

Unit 2

B. Read and write-Let's sing

 夯实基础

一、读下面的语段,请按照时间顺序给它们排序,将数字1—4填在方框里。

| Wow, it's ten o'clock at night. It's time to go to bed. □ | I am hungry. It's time for lunch. I like chicken with tomatoes. □ |

| It is ten o'clock. We like PE class very much. Let's go to the playground and play football. □ | It's 7 o'clock. It is time for breakfast. Let's have some bread and milk. □ |

二、看图,完成下列任务。

任务一:根据图片内容,填写单词或短语,补全对话。

1. A: What time is it?

   B: It's _____. It's time for _____ class.

2. A: What time is it?

   B: It's _____. It's time to _____.

任务二:根据实际情况画出时针和分针,并仿照任务一写对话。

A: _____

B: _____

提升能力

三、读绘本故事,完成下列任务。

①

②

③

It's the first school day. Rabbit and Turtle are ready for school. It is 7 o'clock. Time for breakfast.

It's 7:45 a.m. Time to go to school.

It's 1._____. Time for 2._____.

④

⑤

⑥

It's 3._____. Time for 4._____.

It's 5._____. Time for 6._____.

It's 7._____. Time to 8._____.

任务一:根据图片,从方框中选择合适的选项补全故事,将其序号填在横线上。

A. 5:20 p.m.　　B. 2 p.m.　　C. 8:20 a.m.　　D. 11:50 a.m.
E. lunch　　　　F. go home　　G. art class　　H. English class

任务二:根据故事内容,判断下列句子正误,正确的写"T",错误的写"F"。

(　　)1. The rabbit has an English class and an art class at school.

(　　)2. The turtle has lunch at 11:50 a.m.

(　　)3. The rabbit goes home at 5:20 p.m.

(　　)4. The turtle arrives at(到达) school at 5:20 p.m.

C. Story time

一、根据课文内容判断下列句子正误,正确的打"√",错误的打"×"。

(　　)1. Zoom wakes up at eight o'clock. He is late for school.

(　　)2. It's seven o'clock now.

(　　)3. Today is April Fool's Day.

二、任务型阅读。

Rebecca, Sun Hong, Emily and Lily are friends. But they live in different countries. Rebecca lives in Cairo, Egypt. It is three o'clock in the afternoon now. It is time to play sports. Sun Hong lives in Beijing, China. Beijing is six hours ahead of(早于) Cairo. Emily lives in London, the UK. London is two hours behind(晚于) Cairo. Lily lives in New York, the USA. New York is seven hours behind Cairo.

任务一:根据短文内容,在钟面上画出相应的时间。

1. Cairo   2. Beijing   3. London   4. New York

任务二:根据生活常识以及短文内容完成下列句子或对话。

1. For Sun Hong, it is time to ＿＿＿＿ ＿＿＿＿ ＿＿＿＿ now.

2. In Egypt, it is in the afternoon now. In China, it is in the ＿＿＿＿ now.

   In New York, it is in the ＿＿＿＿ now.

3. —What time is it in other cities? Can you say a different one?

   —It is ＿＿＿＿ ＿＿＿＿ (time) in ＿＿＿＿ (city).

Unit 2 听力训练

一、听对话,选择与你所听到的内容相符的图片,将其序号填入题前括号里。

( )1. A.  B.   C.

( )2. A.  B.  C.

( )3. A.  B.  C.

( )4. A.  B.   C.

二、听录音,选择正确的答语,将其序号填入题前括号里。

( )1. A. It's 9:30.　　　　B. Just a minute.　　　　C. It's time for PE class.

( )2. A. It is the art room.　　　　B. I'm in New York.
　　　C. I want to sleep.

( )3. A. I can read and write.　　　　B. I can sing and dance.
　　　C. I can play basketball.

( )4. A. Yes, it is.　　　　B. Yes, I do.　　　　C. No, it doesn't.

三、听对话,给时钟选择对应的人物及其所在的城市,将其序号填在相应的横线上。

| A. Pedro | B. Mike | C. Amy | D. Oliver |
| a. Sydney | b. Toronto | c. Madrid(马德里) | d. London |

1. 　　2. 　　3. 　　4.

Unit 3 Weather

A. Let's talk   Let's play

夯实基础

一、看图,选择合适的单词补全句子,将其序号填在横线上。

A. cold   B. hot   C. outside   D. careful

1. Be _____ ! The car is coming!

2. The dog is _____ its house.

3. It's _____ today.

4. The water is very _____ .

二、选择正确的答案,将其序号填入题前括号里。

(   ) 1. —What time is it? —_____
   A. It's cold.   B. It's 9:00.   C. It's time for lunch.

(   ) 2. —Can I go home now? —_____
   A. Yes, I can.   B. Yes, you are.   C. No, you can't.

(   ) 3. —Have some milk, Tom. —_____
   A. OK!   B. Be careful!   C. Help yourself!

三、看图,完成下面的对话。

1. —Can I have some _____ ?

   —Yes, _____ .

2. —Can I _____ ?

   —No, _____ .

3. —Can I _____?

   —_____.

提升能力

四、任务型阅读。

任务一：选择合适的句子补全对话，将其序号填在横线上。（有一项多余）

Taotao: 1. _____
Mum: It's 5:00.
Taotao: 2. _____
Mum: No, you can't. 3. _____
Taotao: OK. Can I have some noodles?
Mum: 4. _____ Be careful! They're hot.
Taotao: Can I go outside after dinner?
Mum: 5. _____

A. It's time for dinner.
B. It's time to read books.
C. No, you can't. It's cold today.
D. Mum, what time is it?
E. Can I watch TV now?
F. Yes, you can.

任务二：根据对话内容，判断Taotao是否可以做下列事情，可以做的在括号里打"√"，不可以做的打"×"。

( ) 1. 　　( ) 2. 　　( ) 3.

A. Let's learn　Let's chant

夯实基础

一、判断下列单词与图片是否相符，相符的在括号里写"T"，不相符的写"F"。

1. cold(　)　　2. hot(　)　　3. cool(　)　　4. warm(　)

二、以四月份的天气情况为例,找出描述正确的句子,在括号里打"√"。

(　　)1. It's warm in Kunming. 　　(　　)2. It's cold in Haikou.

(　　)3. It's hot in Changchun. 　　(　　)4. It's warm in Shanghai.

(　　)5. It's hot in Urumqi.

三、看图,选择合适的句子,将其序号填在图片下的括号里。

1.　　　　2.　　　　3.　　　　4.

(　　)　　(　　)　　(　　)　　(　　)

A. It's warm inside. Take off your shoes.

B. It's cold outside. Put on your hat.

C. It's hot today. I want to eat watermelons.

D. It's windy today. Let's fly kites.

提升能力

四、根据提示选择合适的单词,完成天气预报播报稿。

Beijing　20℃　　Lhasa　15℃　　Harbin　5℃　　Hong Kong　30℃

hot　　cool　　warm　　cold

Good morning. This is today's weather report. It's 1._____ in Beijing. It's 2._____ in Lhasa. It's 3._____ in Harbin. It's 4._____ in Hong Kong. That's the weather report for today. Thank you for listening!

A. Let's spell

夯实基础

一、听录音,根据图片补全单词,完成小韵文。

Mr Sh__ __k is playing with his b__ __l.

He gets a c__ __l from Mr H__ __l.

There's a p__ __ty on M__ __s.

Although(虽然) it is so f__ __,

he can drive his super c__ __ and then dance

with Mr H__ __l.

注意 ar 和 al 的发音规律哟!

二、看图,并根据单词画线部分的发音规律填写所缺单词。

1. My brother is _____. He plays with his ball near the _____.

2. This is a card with a _____. That is a card with an _____.

提升能力

三、读一读小怪物们的自我介绍,找出含有与例词画线部分相同发音的单词,将其写在横线上,并根据描述在框中写出它们的名字。

1. Hi, I am Mark. I am a farmer with strong arms. I work hard and I like art. I can draw a pretty garden on the farm.

   bar:_____

2. Hi, I am Fall. I am not tall. I am small. I look like a ball. I like to go to the shopping mall.

   all:_____

Unit 3 阶段复习

听力部分

一、听录音,选择你所听到的单词,将其序号填入题前括号里。

(   )1. A. hot　　　B. hat　　　　(   )2. A. cold　　　B. cool
(   )3. A. warm　　B. water　　　(   )4. A. tall　　　B. ball
(   )5. A. arm　　　B. farm

二、听录音,判断下列图片与你所听到的内容是否相符,相符的在括号里打"√",不相符的打"×"。

1.  (   )
2. 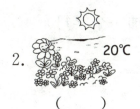 (   )
3.  (   )
4.  (   )

三、听录音,选择正确的答语,将其序号填入题前括号里。

(   )1. A. Yes, it is.　　　　　　　　B. Yes, you can.
(   )2. A. It's 2 p.m.　　　　　　　　B. It's cold.
(   )3. A. Yes. Here you are.　　　　　B. Yes, I can.
(   )4. A. Yes. Put on a hat.　　　　　B. Yes. Take off your hat.
(   )5. A. Yes, it is.　　　　　　　　B. Yes, it's hot.

四、听短文,在表格相应的栏中打"√"。

	A. ❄ −3℃	B. ⛅ 25℃	C. ☀ 30℃	D. 15℃
1. Kunming				
2. Qingdao				
3. Sanya				
4. Shenyang				

读写部分

五、找出每组单词中画线部分发音不同的一项,将其序号填入题前括号里。

(   )1. A. f<u>ar</u>m　　　B. w<u>ar</u>m　　　C. h<u>ar</u>m

(   )2. A. ha<u>l</u>f　　　B. ba<u>ll</u>　　　C. ta<u>l</u>k

(   )3. A. w<u>ar</u>　　　B. c<u>ar</u>　　　C. <u>ar</u>t

(   )4. A. f<u>ar</u>　　　B. qu<u>ar</u>ter　　　C. c<u>ar</u>d

六、根据文字提示,在四线三格里填写正确的关于天气的单词。

1. not(改变其中一个字母)

2. fool(改变其中一个字母)

3. arm(添加一个字母)

4. old(添加一个字母)

七、选择正确的答案,将其序号填入题前括号里。

(   )1. Good morning. This is the _____.

　　　A. report weather　　B. weather report　　C. weather

(   )2. _____ The soup is hot.

　　　A. Wake up!　　B. Hurry up!　　C. Be careful!

(   )3. —Can I go outside now? —_____

　　　A. Yes, I can.　　B. Yes, you can.　　C. No, I don't.

(   )4. It's warm today. You can _____ your hat.

　　　A. put on　　B. take off　　C. put

八、选择合适的句子补全对话,将其序号填在横线上。

Sarah: 1. _____

Mum: It's 7:00.

Sarah: 2. _____

Mum: Yes, you can. It's cold outside. 3. _____

Sarah: 4. _____

A. OK, Mum.
B. What time is it, Mum?
C. Can I go outside?
D. Please put on your hat.

九、任务型阅读。

It's hot. He wears a T-shirt.

He wears shorts.

He has an ice cream.

It's rainy. She wears a raincoat.

She wears rain boots.

She has an umbrella.

It's cold. She wears a coat.

She wears snow boots.

She has a sled.

任务一:读一读,找出文中的一对反义词写在下面的横线上。

_____ _____

任务二:根据图文信息,将下列图片连线。

1.   2.   3.

A.   B.   C.

任务三:根据图文信息,判断下列句子正误,正确的在括号里写"T",错误的写"F"。

(   )1. It is hot. The boy wears a T-shirt and shorts.

(   )2. It is rainy. The girl wears a raincoat and snow boots.

(   )3. It is cold. The girl wears a coat and rain boots.

B. Let's talk   Let's play

夯实基础

一、观察这款天气预报应用软件上的信息，根据首字母提示，在四线三格中补全单词。

1. It's c_____ and w_____ in Beijing.

2. It's s_____ and h_____ in Singapore City.

3. It's r_____ and c_____ in Sydney.

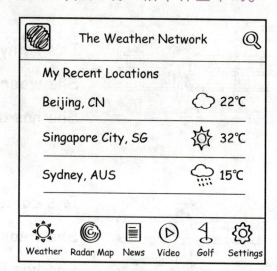

二、选择与图片相符的句子完成对话，将其序号填入题前括号里。

( )1. —_____
　　—Yes, it is.
　　A. Is it cool?　　B. Is it warm?
　　C. Is it hot?

( )2. —Is it cold?
　　—_____
　　A. No. It's thirty-two degrees today.
　　B. No. It's twenty-three degrees today.
　　C. No. It's thirty degrees today.

( )3. —_____
　　—It's cloudy and cold.
　　A. What's the weather like in Paris?
　　B. What's the weather like in Toronto?
　　C. What's the weather like in London?

Unit 3

提升能力

三、任务型阅读。

（Five friends are on the video call...）

Li Wei：Hello, my dear friends! It is a sunny day today in Beijing. I can feel everything is very warm. What's the weather like in your cities?

Andy：It is rainy in London today. How about Moscow, Nina? Is it cold?

Nina：Yes, it is. And it is snowy outside now. Bruce, is it cold in Sydney, too?

Bruce：No, it isn't. It is cloudy today. It is cool.

Annie：It is windy in New York today. I can fly my kite!

任务一：根据对话内容，连线。

1. Beijing   2. London   3. Moscow   4. Sydney   5. New York

A. 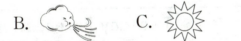　B. 　C. 　D. 　E.

任务二：根据对话内容，回答问题。

—Can Nina fly a kite today? —_____

任务三：根据你的实际情况，补全下面的句子。

I live in _____. It is _____ and _____ today.

B. Let's learn　Let's play

夯实基础

一、判断下列句子与图片是否相符，相符的在括号里写"T"，不相符的写"F"。

(　　)1. It's cloudy.　　(　　)2. It's rainy.　　(　　)3. It's sunny.

37

( )4. It's snowy.   ( )5. It's windy.

二、看图，完成下面的句子或对话。

1. —Is it cold?
   —_____, _____ _____.

2. —What's the weather like in _____?
   —It's _____ and _____.

3. It's _____ and _____ in _____.

提升能力

三、根据表格中各城市一月份某几天的天气信息，选择正确的答案。

	Monday（星期一）	Two-day Forecast（预报）
Changchun	-18℃--4℃ snowy	Tuesday -12℃--5℃ ☀ Wednesday -15℃--4℃
Sanya	18℃-27℃ cloudy	Tuesday 19℃-29℃ ☀ Wednesday 18℃-25℃
Nanjing	5℃-11℃ cloudy	Tuesday 4℃-10℃ 🌧 Wednesday 3℃-9℃

( )1. It's _____ in Changchun on Monday.
   A. sunny   B. cloudy   C. snowy

( )2. Take your _____ on Tuesday and Wednesday in Nanjing.
   A. ball   B. umbrella   C. pen

( )3. It's cloudy in _____ and _____ on Monday.
   A. Changchun; Sanya   B. Sanya; Nanjing   C. Changchun; Nanjing

( )4. You can _____ in _____ on Tuesday.
   A. fly a kite; Changchun   B. make a snowman; Nanjing
   C. swim; Sanya

B. Read and write-Let's sing

夯实基础

一、为下列对话选择合适的图片，在相应的圆圈里打"√"。

1. —Dad, is it warm today? Can I play outside?
   —Yes, you can. It's warm outside.

2. —Hello, Mike! What's the weather like there?
   —It's cloudy here.

3. —Mum, can I have some tea?
   —Yes, but it's hot. Be careful.

4. —Mum, can I go outside?
   —No. It's snowy and cold outside.

二、按要求完成下列各题。

1. It's _____ and _____ today.（看图补全句子）

2. It's _____ in Harbin.（看图补全句子）

3. outside, is, cold, It （.）（连词成句）
   _____

4. weather, is, like, What, today, the （?）（连词成句）
   _____

提升能力

三、任务型阅读。

It is cold and snowy in Beijing today. I can make a snowman. But in Sydney, it's hot and sunny. People have to put on their sunglasses(太阳镜). They can swim in the water. It's "cool"!

任务一：阅读短文，判断下列句子正误，正确的在括号里写"T"，错误的写"F"。

( )1. It's cold and windy in Beijing today. I can make a snowman.

( )2. In Sydney, people have to put on their sunglasses, because it is sunny and hot today.

( )3. In Beijing, people can wear T-shirts today.

任务二：根据短文内容，填写所缺单词或短语，完成表格。

City	Weather	Activity（活动）
Beijing	cold and 1._____	2._____
3._____	4._____ and 5._____	go swimming

四、读绘本故事，完成下列任务。

 ① "It's going to snow," says the postman.

 ② "It's going to snow," says the farmer.

 ③ It snows. The postman has a bad fall and breaks(弄折) his leg.

 ④ It snows. The farmer's donkeys get hungry more easily(更容易).

 ⑤ There is no school today—an extra(额外的) day off. Children have snowball fights. They make snowmen and build snow houses.

任务一：读绘本故事，判断下列句子正误，正确的写"T"，错误的写"F"。

( )1. It is a snowy day.

( )2. The farmer and the postman are happy when it snows.

任务二：再读绘本故事，补全孩子们在雪天进行的活动，并试着画出其中一个孩子的表情。

1. have _____ fights
2. make _____
3. build _____ houses

任务三：根据绘本故事，请思考"Is a snowy day good or not?"，并试着写出一条理由。

_____

C. Story time

一、选择合适的单词补全句子，将其序号填在横线上。

1. It will be _____ in Dalian.
2. You look _____.
3. Ah-choo! It's cold _____.
4. _____ you!

A. Bless   B. warm
C. terrible   D. here

二、任务型阅读。

It is snowy outside. Jack plays in the white snow so happily. But he runs too fast, so he falls down（摔倒）and loses his keys in the snow. He can't find the keys. He asks Dad for help. Dad says, "Oh, I can't help you. The snow is too deep（深的）. But we can wait! Something big and yellow will come out soon. It can help you find the keys."

任务一：选择正确的答案，将其序号填入题前括号里。

( )1. Why can't Jack and his dad find the keys?
    A. Because it's snowy today.   B. Because Jack runs too fast.
    C. Because the snow is too deep.

( )2. What can help Jack find the keys?
    A. An egg.   B. The sun.   C. The wind.

任务二：根据实际情况回答问题。

Can you think of other ways to help Jack find the keys?

_____

Unit 3 听力训练

一、听录音,圈出相应的单词。

二、听录音,选择正确的答语,将其序号填入题前括号里。

(　　)1. A. He's from Canada.　　B. She's OK.　　C. It's warm and sunny.

(　　)2. A. No, it isn't.　　B. Yes. It's cool.　　C. No. It's warm.

(　　)3. A. Here he comes.　　B. Sorry, you can't. It's cold today.

　　　　C. Have some soup.

(　　)4. A. I'm fine, thank you.　　B. It's cloudy.　　C. It's time for dinner.

(　　)5. A. It's 30 degrees, too.　　B. I can swim.　　C. I can fly my kite.

三、听短文,给下列城市选择相应的天气,将图片序号填入相应的括号里。

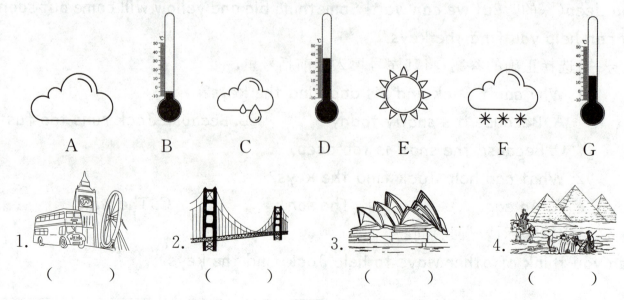

Unit 4 At the farm

A. Let's talk   Let's play

夯实基础

一、根据单词选择相应的图片，将其序号填入题前括号里。

(　　)1. these　　　A. 　　　B.

(　　)2. carrot　　　A.　　　B.

(　　)3. tomatoes　　　A.　　　B.

(　　)4. yum　　　A.　　　B.

二、找出每组单词中不同类的一项，将其序号填入题前括号里。

(　　)1. A. try　　　B. these　　　C. look

(　　)2. A. yellow　　　B. blue　　　C. yum

(　　)3. A. tomato　　　B. apples　　　C. carrot

(　　)4. A. some　　　B. good　　　C. big

三、为下列蔬菜或水果选择相应的颜色，将其序号填入题前括号里。

(　　)1.　　　A. They are green.

(　　)2.　　　B. They are red.

(　　)3.　　　C. They are orange.

提升能力

四、根据图片,选择合适的选项完成 Zip 和 Zoom 的对话,在相应的括号里打"√"。

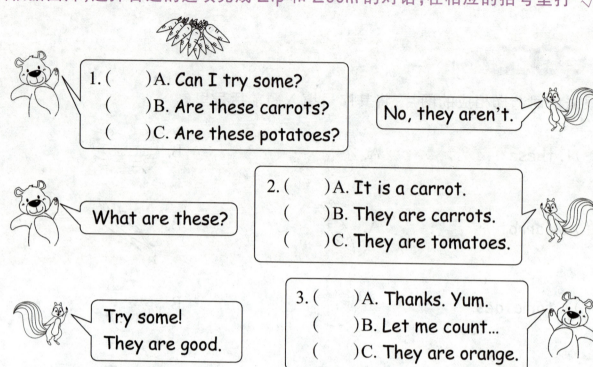

1. ( ) A. Can I try some?
   ( ) B. Are these carrots?
   ( ) C. Are these potatoes?

   No, they aren't.

   What are these?

2. ( ) A. It is a carrot.
   ( ) B. They are carrots.
   ( ) C. They are tomatoes.

   Try some!
   They are good.

3. ( ) A. Thanks. Yum.
   ( ) B. Let me count…
   ( ) C. They are orange.

A. Let's learn   Let's chant

夯实基础

一、根据图片提示,补全单词或短语。

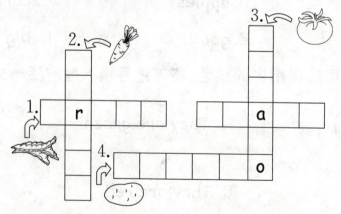

二、圈出正确的单词补全句子。

1. The green beans (is/are) green and (long/tall).

2. Rabbits like (apples/carrots). (It's/They're) orange.

3. Look at these (potato/potatoes).
4. I like (tomatoes/tomato).
5. The (onion/onions) make (my/me) cry.

三、判断下列图片与对话是否相符,相符的在括号里打"√",不相符的打"×"。

( )1. —What are these?
　　　—They're tomatoes and potatoes. I love to eat them.

( )2. —Are these carrots?　—Yes, they are.
　　　—How many?　—Four.

( )3. —Are they green beans?
　　　—No, they aren't. They're onions.

提升能力

四、任务型阅读。

　　My name is Tim. Welcome to my home. Let me show you the fridge. Look at these tomatoes. They are red and round. My sister likes them very much. But I don't like them. I like potatoes. They are brown and big. My father likes onions. My mother loves to eat green beans. These green beans are so long. The carrots are good. Nina will try them for dinner. Who is Nina? It's the rabbit over there. It is very cute.

任务一:根据短文内容,将下列人或动物与其喜欢的食物连线。

1. 　2. 　3. 　4. 　5.
　　　　　　　　　　　　　Tim

A. 　B. 　C. 　D. 　E. 🥔

任务二:仿照短文内容,补全句子,写一种你喜欢吃的食物。
I _____. They _____.

A. Let's spell

夯实基础

一、听录音,选择你所听到的单词,将其序号填入题前括号里。

( )1. A. fork   B. work   ( )2. A. world   B. worth
( )3. A. forty   B. short   ( )4. A. horse   B. north
( )5. A. for   B. born   ( )6. A. housework   B. homework

二、根据字母组合 or 的发音给下列单词或短语归类,将其序号填在横线上。

```
A. short      B. world       C. born       D. sport
E. word       F. New York    G. work       H. forty
```

1. horse：_____   2. homework：_____

三、根据句意选择相应的图片,将其序号填入题前括号里。

( )1. I have a storybook.
( )2. This is New York. It is a big city.
( )3. Do you know this word "pig"?
( )4. There are 40 students in my class.

提升能力

四、看图并读一读,根据画线部分的发音规律,在四线三格上写出所缺单词。

1. I use a sh<u>or</u>t _____ to eat the pork.

2. Corn does sports near his _____.

3. Her _____ is to write these words.

Unit 4 阶段复习

听力部分

一、听录音,选择你所听到的内容,将其序号填入题前括号里。

( )1. A. these   B. they   C. try

( )2. A. carrot   B. cat   C. cry

( )3. A. What are these?   B. What's this?   C. What are they?

( )4. A. Are these potatoes?   B. Are these tomatoes?
      C. Are these onions?

( )5. A. They're so big!   B. They're so good!   C. They're so long!

二、听录音,判断下列图片与你所听到的内容是否相符,相符的打"√",不相符的打"×"。

1.   2.  3.   4.  5.

( )   ( )   ( )   ( )   ( )

三、听对话,将人物与其喜欢的食物连线。

1.   2.  3.

A.  B.  C.

四、听短文,判断下列句子正误,正确的写"T",错误的写"F"。

( )1. My grandpa has a farm.   ( )2. The tomatoes are red and big.

( )3. The potatoes are brown.   ( )4. There are no green beans.

( )5. The carrots are good for my eyes.

读写部分

五、选择与每组单词同类的一项,将其序号填入题前括号里。

( )1. purple   brown   yellow

( )2. tomato   potato   onion

( )3. watermelon   pear   orange

( )4. small   long   short

A. apple
B. blue
C. big
D. carrot

六、选择正确的答案,将其序号填入题前括号里。

( )1. The _____ are big.

    A. potato   B. potatos   C. potatoes

( )2. _____ I will try.

    A. Carrots   B. carrots   C. carrot

( )3. I like _____.

    A. Green beans   B. green beans   C. green bean

( )4. —What are they? —_____

    A. It's a tomato.   B. I like tomatoes.   C. They are tomatoes.

七、按要求完成下列各题。

1. The _____ are red.(看图补全句子)

2. The _____ are so long.(看图补全句子)

3. I like to eat _____.(看图补全句子)

4. carrots, Are, these (?)(连词成句)

_____

5. are, What, these (?)(连词成句)

_____

八、看图，完成下列任务。

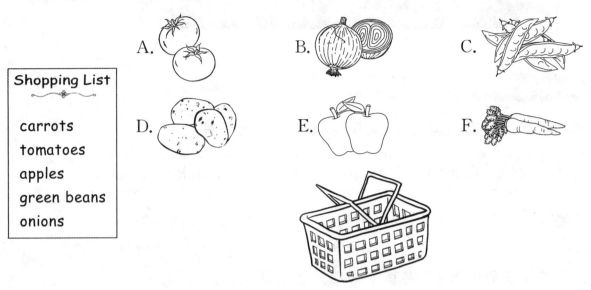

Shopping List
carrots
tomatoes
apples
green beans
onions

任务一：根据购物清单，将妈妈要买的蔬果用线连入购物篮里。

任务二：根据常识，从购物清单中选词填空（注意用单词的适当形式）。

1. _____ are orange in colour and good for our eyes.

2. An _____ a day keeps the doctor away.

九、任务型阅读。

 1. I like vegetables.
Vegetables are healthy.
I'm cutting _____.

 2. I like vegetables.
Vegetables are delicious.
I'm eating _____.

 3. I like vegetables.
Vegetables are tasty.
I'm cutting _____.

 4. I like vegetables.
Vegetables are good for me. I'm eating _____.

任务一：根据图片选择合适的单词或短语，将其序号填在横线上。

A. green beans   B. potatoes   C. onions   D. carrots

任务二：根据上述内容，判断下列句子正误，正确的在括号里写"T"，错误的写"F"。

( )1. Vegetables are healthy and delicious.

( )2. The boy doesn't like vegetables.

( )3. Vegetables are tasty.

B. Let's talk   Let's play

夯实基础

一、为下列动物选择相应的声音,将其序号填入题前括号里。

A. quack   B. moo   C. neigh   D. woof   E. cluck   F. meow

(   )1. dog   (   )2. hen   (   )3. cat
(   )4. cow   (   )5. duck   (   )6. horse

二、根据情景选择正确的答案,将其序号填入题前括号里。

(   )1. What are those?
A. There are horses.
B. They are horses.
C. They are cows.

(   )2. Are they dogs?
A. Yes, it is.
B. Yes, they are.
C. No, they aren't. They are cats.

(   )3. Mmm... Eight.
A. Are they ducks?
B. What are those?
C. How many ducks do you see?

三、结合图片,用数字给下列句子排序,使其组成一段通顺的对话。

(   ) How many horses do you have?
(   ) Wow! You have a lot of animals! What are those?
(   ) No, they aren't. They're hens.
(   ) Mmm... Eleven.
(   ) They're horses.
(   ) What about these? Are they ducks?

提升能力

四、选择合适的句子补全对话，将其序号填在横线上。（有一项多余）

Mike: Look! 1. _____

John: Guess!

Mike: Are they hens?

John: 2. _____

Mike: Are they ducks?

John: 3. _____

Mike: 4. _____

John: I have four.

A. How many ducks do you have?
B. Yes, they are.
C. No, they aren't.
D. Are they cows?
E. What are those, John?

B. Let's learn   Draw and say

夯实基础

一、尽可能多地圈出表示动物的单词。

h	n	s	c	a	t
d	o	g	h	i	h
s	h	e	e	p	o
j	f	a	n	i	r
d	u	c	k	g	s
q	c	o	w	r	e

二、看图，完成下面的对话。

1. —What are they?

   —They are _____.

2. —How many sheep are there?

   —There are _____.

3. —Are those hens?

—No, they _____. They are _____.

4. —What are those?

—_____.

三、按要求完成下列各题。

1. cute, They, so, are （!）(连词成句)

2. horses, have, many, you, How, do （?）(连词成句)

3. They're hens.（改为一般疑问句）

4. They're <u>ducks</u>.（对画线部分提问）

提升能力

四、看图，判断下列句子的描述是否正确，正确的在括号里写"T"，错误的写"F"。

(　　)1. It is rainy and cool today.

(　　)2. There are six hens on the farm.

(　　)3. We can see five cows on the farm.

(　　)4. Four horses are running on the farm.

(　　)5. The girl has two big sheep and three little sheep.

B. Read and write-Let's sing

夯实基础

一、选择正确的单词补全句子，将其写在横线上。

1. There _____ (is/are) a red tomato.

2. _____ (It/They) are dogs.

3. How many _____ (goat/sheep) do you have?

4. Mr MacDonald _____ (have/has) a farm.

二、判断下列句子与图片是否相符，相符的在括号里打"√"，不相符的打"×"。

1. (　　) This is the vegetable garden.
   (　　) These are tomatoes.

2. (　　) There are many animals on the farm.
   (　　) There are four sheep and five ducks.

3. (　　) They are goats.
   (　　) There is lots of grass(草).

提升能力

三、仿照例子写句子，并试着画一画，再写一写。

例：These are sheep.
　　Those are horses.

1. _____

2. _____

四、读绘本故事，完成下列任务。

任务一：读绘本故事，写出所缺单词。

任务二：根据绘本故事判断下列句子正误，正确的写"T"，错误的写"F"。

( ) 1. Rabbit likes pumpkins.

( ) 2. Rabbit buys pumpkins for Pig.

( ) 3. Pig doesn't buy carrots.

( ) 4. Pig and Rabbit are friends.

C. Story time

一、选择合适的单词补全句子，将其序号填在横线上。

A. make　　B. They　　C. Good　　D. are
E. hungry　F. at　　　G. mutton　H. don't

1. Look _____ the vegetables.
2. I _____ like vegetables.
3. What _____ those?
4. _____ are cows.
5. I like _____.
6. Let's _____ a hat.
7. _____ idea!
8. I'm _____.

二、请根据十二生肖里的动物及其顺序，完成下列任务。

任务一：按照十二生肖里动物的顺序，填上缺失动物的名称。

Rat→Ox→1._____→2._____→Dragon→Snake→3._____→
4._____→Monkey→Rooster→5._____→6._____

任务二：圈出下列不属于十二生肖的动物。

A.　　　B. 　　　C. 　　　D.

E. 　　　F. 　　　G. 　　　H.

I. 　　　J. 　　　K. 　　　L.

任务三：根据你的实际情况回答问题。

What is your birth-year animal(生肖)? Why?

_____

Unit 4 听力训练

一、听录音,选择你所听到的单词,将其序号填入题前括号里。

( )1. A. horse   B. house   ( )2. A. now   B. cow

( )3. A. sheep   B. sleep   ( )4. A. these   B. this

( )5. A. tomatoes   B. potatoes

二、听对话,选择与你所听到的内容相符的图片,将其序号填入题前括号里。

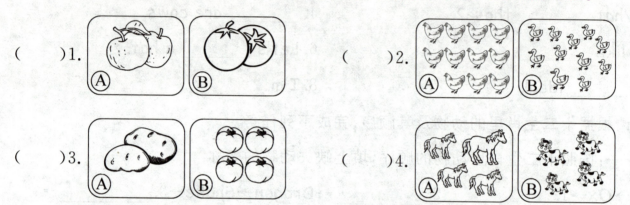

三、听录音,选择正确的答语,将其序号填入题前括号里。

( )1. A. Yes, it is.   B. Yes, they are.   C. No. They're sheep.

( )2. A. They're white and purple.   B. It's white.
       C. They're red.

( )3. A. They're cows.   B. This is my sister.   C. It's a cow.

( )4. A. Yes, it is.   B. No, they aren't.   C. It's a tomato.

( )5. A. It's a horse.   B. They're horses.   C. Those are horses.

四、听短文,判断下列句子正误,正确的写"T",错误的写"F"。

( )1. This is my father's farm.

( )2. We can't see tomatoes on the farm.

( )3. There are two horses on the farm.

( )4. We can see many vegetables and fruit on the farm.

( )5. The farm is big and nice.

Unit 5 My clothes

A. Let's talk   Let's play

夯实基础

一、选择正确的答案,将其序号填入题前括号里。

(　　)1.　—Is this John's?　—_____
　　　　A. Yes, it is.　　　B. No. It's John's.　　　C. No, he isn't.

(　　)2.　—Are these yours?　—_____
　　　　A. No, it isn't.　　B. Yes, it's Amy's.　　　C. No, they aren't.

(　　)3.　—What time is it?　—_____
　　　　A. It's six time.　　B. It's six o'clock.　　　C. This is six.

二、判断下列对话与图片是否相符,相符的在括号里打"√",不相符的打"×"。

(　　)1.　—What colour are your shoes?
　　　　—They are white.

白色

(　　)2.　—Are those your pencils?
　　　　—No. They are Amy's.

Alice's

(　　)3.　—What are they?
　　　　—They are hats.

三、看图,完成下面的对话。

1. Mike: Are these books yours, Zhang Peng?
   Zhang Peng: No, _____.
   　　　　　　They're _____.

   John

2. Zoom: Is this bag Amy's?
   Zip: No, _____.
   　　　It's _____.

   Chen Jie

3. Amy: Are these rulers yours, Sarah?
   Sarah: _____.

   Sarah

57

提升能力

四、看图,根据图片提示,从方框中选择正确的单词填写在四线三格中。

| ape's(猿的) | Whose |
| giraffe's | is |

A: Eyes can help you tell one animal from another. Look at these pictures!

B: 1. _____ eyes are these? Are these eyes the 2. _____?

A: Yes, they are.

B: Whose eye 3. _____ this?

A: It is the 4. _____.

A. Let's learn   Let's do

夯实基础

一、根据图片提示,在字母串中圈出正确的单词,并将其抄写在四线三格中。

1. kedresspo   2. grqhatf   3. qdpantssy   4. jskirtsy

二、看图，选择合适的句子，将其序号填入图下括号里。

1. (　　)　　2. (　　)　　3. (　　)　　4. (　　)　　5.  (　　)

A. Wash your skirt.　　B. Hang up your dress.　　C. Take off your hat.
D. Put away your pants.　　E. Put on your shirt.

三、根据图片信息和提示，仿照例子写句子。

例：   I like <u>this</u> hat. I like <u>these</u> hats.

1. I like _____ _____. I like _____ dresses.（that/those）

2. _____.
_____.
（this/these）

提升能力

四、读对话，将人物与他们各自的物品匹配，将其序号填在横线上。

Cici：Wow, so many beautiful clothes on the teacher's desk. Why?

Miss Brown：They are for our Chinese writing class. Clothes tell stories.

Cici：Oh, yes. That dress looks so traditional(传统的). I like it.

Miss Brown：It's made of silk(丝绸). It's Chen Jie's. Her mother went to Hangzhou last weekend. It's a gift. Oh, these are Amy's. They're her birthday gifts, a blouse and a hat. And this cap is Wu Yifan's. His grandpa's signature(签名) is on it. His grandpa is a scientist(科学家).

Chen Jie：_____　　Amy：_____　　Wu Yifan：_____

A. 　　B. 　　C. 　　D.

A. Let's spell

夯实基础

一、听录音,结合图片及字母组合 le 的发音规则补全单词。

Twinkle, twink_ _, lit_ _ _ star.

Unc_ _ Tur_ _ _ chants to his son,

"Little Bee lights a can_ _ _.

Mr Ea_ _ _ flies in the sky…"

二、判断下列每组单词画线部分的发音是否相同,相同的打"√",不相同的打"×"。

(　　)1. app<u>le</u>　　　lemon　　　(　　)2. <u>le</u>t　　　litt<u>le</u>

(　　)3. <u>le</u>ft　　　<u>le</u>g　　　(　　)4. purp<u>le</u>　　　peop<u>le</u>

三、看图,完成下面的句子。

1. This is my new _____.

2. There are four _____ in Tom's family. They are

Tom's parents, Tom's _____ brother and Tom.

提升能力

四、根据短文内容或图片提示补全单词,并体会字母组合 le 在单词中的发音规律。

　　Seatt<u>le</u> is a city(城市) of the USA. There are over 4,000,000 peop_ _.

This is the Space Need_ _ 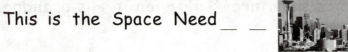. There is a bicyc_ _ race

 every year to another American city, Portland.

60

Unit 5 阶段复习

听力部分

一、听录音,选择你所听到的单词,将其序号填入题前括号里。

( )1. A. clothes   B. coat   ( )2. A. shirt   B. skirt

( )3. A. whose   B. shoes   ( )4. A. apple   B. people

( )5. A. table   B. little

二、听录音,选择与你所听到的内容相符的图片,将其序号填入题前括号里。

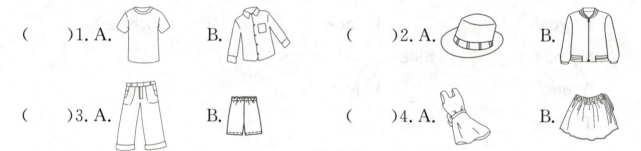

三、听对话,从方框中选择下列物品对应的主人的名字,将其序号填入题前括号里。

A. Chen Jie   B. Sarah   C. Mike

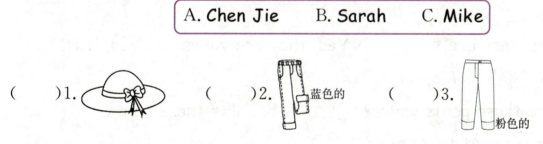

四、听对话,找出下列物品所在的房间,将其序号标在相应房间的空白处。

A. dress   B. hat   C. shoes   D. skirt

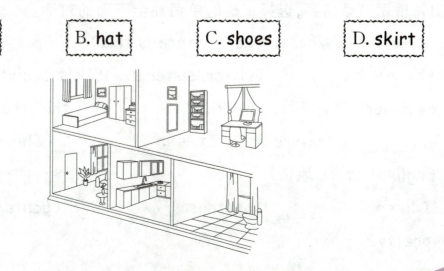

读写部分

五、找出每组单词中不同类的一项,将其序号填入题前括号里。

(　　)1. A. black　　　　B. dress　　　　C. brown

(　　)2. A. what　　　　B. where　　　　C. hat

(　　)3. A. clothes　　　B. sweater　　　C. skirt

(　　)4. A. this　　　　B. time　　　　C. that

(　　)5. A. yours　　　　B. four　　　　C. eight

六、选择正确的答案,将其序号填入题前括号里。

(　　)1. I can _____ my shirt.

　　　A. wash　　　　B. look　　　　C. white

(　　)2. My pants _____ blue.

　　　A. am　　　　B. is　　　　C. are

(　　)3. They are _____ hats.

　　　A. Mike　　　　B. Mike's　　　　C. Mike is

(　　)4. —Are these shoes yours?

　　　—_____

　　　A. Yes, they are.　　B. Yes, they are yours.　　C. Yes, it is.

(　　)5. —_____ —Me, too.

　　　A. Are these pants yours?　　B. I like these pants.

　　　C. What about these pants?

七、看图并根据对话内容,选择正确的单词补全下面的对话。

Linda: 1. _____(Whose/Who) picture is this?

Lucy: It's my 2. _____(sister/sister's). She's a clothes designer(设计师). I like 3. _____(this/these) 4. _____(dress/skirt). It is in 5. _____(Chinese/English) style(风格).

Linda: I like 6. _____(that/those) 7. _____(pants/shoes). They are pretty.

八、选择合适的句子补全对话，将其序号填在横线上。（有一项多余）

Lily: Tim, please help me put away the school things.

Tim: OK, Lily. Is this your book?

Lily: No, it isn't. 1._____

Tim: 2._____

Lily: Yes, it is.

Tim: Are these pens yours?

Lily: No, they aren't. 3._____

A. Is this your ruler?
B. Are these pencils yours?
C. They are Bill's.
D. It's Andy's.

九、任务型阅读。

Today is Children's Day. Everyone has a gift. Mike has blue pants. Amy has a red dress. Sarah has a green skirt. John has a yellow cap. And Chen Jie has a pink hat. Everyone is happy.

任务一：根据短文内容，将小朋友与他们的礼物连线，并涂上相应的颜色。

1. 2. 3.  4.  5.

A. B. C.  D.  E.

任务二：六一儿童节你收到了什么礼物呢？它是什么颜色的？仿照短文中的句子写一写！

Word Bank

toy car, toy bear, pen, bag, cap, book, dress, ball, hat…

red, pink, black, white, brown, orange…

I have a(n) _____.

B. Let's talk Let's find out

夯实基础

一、选择合适的单词补全句子或对话,将其序号填在横线上。

1. —Is that your pencil, John? —Yes, it's _____.
2. —Is this _____ ruler? —No, it isn't. It's Liu Fang's.
3. —Are those books _____? —Yes, they are.
4. They are _____ new teachers.

A. mine
B. yours
C. your
D. my

二、选择合适的句子补全对话,将其序号填在横线上。(有一项多余)

Amy: Is this your T-shirt?
John: 1. _____ It's my dad's.
Amy: Is this your sister's skirt?
John: 2. _____
Amy: It's very beautiful. Look! Whose shoes are these? They are so small.
John: 3. _____
Amy: 4. _____
John: Yes, they are. They're new.

A. They're my baby brother's.
B. Whose pants are those?
C. Are those your pants?
D. No, it isn't.
E. Yes, it is.

提升能力

三、根据表格内容补全或仿写对话。

	1.	2.	3.	4.
Tina			✓	
Mike		✓		
David				✓
Jane	✓			

1. Miss White: Whose _____ is it?

   Jane: It's _____.

2. Miss White: _____

   Jane: _____

3. Miss White: Whose _____ are these?

   Jane: They're _____.

4. Miss White: _____

   Jane: _____

B. Let's learn   Let's find out

夯实基础

一、选择正确的答案,将其序号填入题前括号里。

(   )1. —Mum, where _____ my socks?

   —They are on the chair.

   A. am   B. is   C. are

(   )2. —What colour are they? —_____

   A. They are white.   B. It's white.   C. They are shorts.

(   )3. —_____ —I want to wear my red shoes.

   A. What are these?   B. What are those?

   C. What do you want to wear?

65

二、根据不同的天气状况选择最合适的衣物,将其序号填入题前括号里。

A. shorts   B. sweater   C. shirt   D. coat   E. jacket

(　　)1. It is sunny today, but it is not so hot. It's just 22 degrees. It is a warm day. I can put on my _____.

(　　)2. It is sunny and very hot today. I can eat an ice cream. I can put on my _____.

(　　)3. It is cloudy and cool today, but there's no wind outside. It's 18 degrees. I can put on my _____.

(　　)4. It is cool today. And the wind is strong outside. It's 15 degrees. I can put on my _____.

(　　)5. It's snowy and very cold outside. I can put on my _____.

提升能力

三、阅读短文,选择正确的答案,将其序号填入题前括号里。

My name is Milly. I'm from Canada. I have some new friends in China. I like their clothes. Look! The skirt is blue. It's Amy's. I like Zhan Fuyi's yellow jacket. There is a panda on it. The girl next to me wears a purple dress. She is Lan Yuxuan. I like my green coat and white skirt. My mum bought(买) them for me yesterday.

(　　)1. Amy has a blue _____.

　　　A.　　　　　　　　B.　　　　　　　　C.

(　　)2. Zhan Fuyi's _____ is yellow.

　　　A.　　　　　　　　B.　　　　　　　　C.

(　　)3. _____ has a purple dress.

　　　A. Milly　　　　B. Zhan Fuyi　　　　C. Lan Yuxuan

(　　)4. _____ is not mentioned(未被提及) by Milly.

　　　A. The white sweater   B. The green coat   C. The white skirt

Unit 5

B. Read and write-Let's sing

夯实基础

一、选择正确的答案,将其序号填入题前括号里。

(   )1. —Is this your sweater? —_____
   A. No, it is.　　　B. Yes, they are.　　　C. No, it isn't.

(   )2. Those socks are _____.
   A. your sister　　B. your sister's　　　C. your sisters

(   )3. —Amy, are those socks yours? —_____
   A. Yes, it is.　　　B. They're red.　　　C. Yes, they are mine.

(   )4. _____ are my clothes.
   A. This　　　　　B. That　　　　　　C. These

二、仿照例子写句子。

例：These are Eric's shoes.

1. _____

例：This is Chen Jie's dress.

2. _____

提升能力

三、任务型阅读。

Hi! My name is Alice. Welcome to my home. Look! This yellow hat is my mother's. It is beautiful. That white shirt is my father's. It is very clean. That red dress is my baby sister's. It is so cute! These blue shorts are mine. I wear them on sunny and hot days. This is my purple jacket. I like its colour.

任务一：阅读短文，给人物选择相应的物品，将其序号填入题前括号里。

(　　)1. Mother　　(　　)2. Father　　(　　)3. Sister　　(　　)4. Alice

A.　　B.　　C.　　D.　　E.

任务二：根据短文内容，判断下列句子正误，正确的在括号里写"T"，错误的写"F"。

(　　)1. The hat is yellow and beautiful.

(　　)2. The shirt is blue and clean.

(　　)3. The dress is red and cute.

(　　)4. Alice likes her purple shorts.

四、阅读下面的文章，完成下列任务。

People wear warm clothes to keep warm. It is cold in many places in winter. What clothes do children there wear?

Iqaluit(伊魁特) is a city near the North Pole(北极). It is very cold in January(一月). It is frozen(结冰的) everywhere. Children wear thick coats and mittens(连指手套). The hood(兜帽) of the coat can keep their heads warm. The mittens can keep their hands warm.

Nepal(尼泊尔) is in South Asia(南亚). It is cold in the north of Nepal in January, too. Children wear hats, scarves and robes(长袍). They are made of yak wool(牦牛毛). The robes have no hoods. The hats and scarves can keep their heads warm.

任务一：根据文章内容，判断下列句子正误，正确的写"T"，错误的写"F"。

(　　)1. It is cold in Iqaluit in January.

(　　)2. Coats in Iqaluit are made of yak wool.

任务二：对比两地的服饰，在表格相应的栏里打"√"。

	robes made of yak wool	coats	hats	mittens	scarves
Iqaluit					
The northern area (地区) of Nepal					

C. Story time

一、选择合适的单词补全句子，将其序号填在横线上。

A. for   B. First   C. having   D. two   E. something   F. me

1. We're _____ a party at school.

2. _____, tie these.

3. Let _____ help you.

4. Then cut _____ small holes for my eyes.

5. Now let me draw _____ on it.

6. Cut two big holes _____ my arms.

二、读故事，完成下列各题。

It's a snowy and cold day. The Little Match Girl is sitting on the ground. Her feet are bare. She is wearing her grandma's big and old dress. She feels so cold and hungry. She misses her grandma so much. Suddenly, her grandma comes and takes her away.

(　　) 1. The word "bare" in this passage means "_____".
　　A. without any hats　　B. without any coats　　C. without any shoes

(　　) 2. Whose dress is the Little Match Girl wearing?
　　A. Her aunt's.　　B. Her grandma's.　　C. Her mother's.

3. According to the passage (根据短文内容), what does the Little Match Girl need?

_____

Unit 5 听力训练

一、听录音,根据所听内容,更改一个字母,写出新单词。

例:bottle→mottle　　1. cattle→＿attle　　2. net＿＿→＿＿＿＿

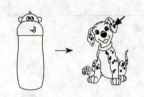  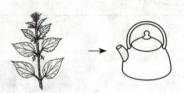

二、听对话,圈出与你所听到的内容相符的图片。

1. A.　　　　B.　　　　2. A.　　　　B.

3. A.　　　　B.　　　　4. A.　　　　B.

三、听录音,选择正确的答语,将其序号填入题前括号里。

(　　)1. A. Red.　　　　　　　B. Of course.　　　　C. Goodbye.
(　　)2. A. These are socks.　　B. It's mine.　　　　C. They're mine.
(　　)3. A. It's on your bed.　　B. It's a pink dress.　　C. Watch out!
(　　)4. A. No, they aren't.　　B. Yes. It's Sam's.　　C. My shorts are nice.
(　　)5. A. No. It's mine.　　　B. Yes, they are.　　　C. Yes, it is.

四、听对话,仿照例子划去这次旅行不需要的衣服,并给所需的衣服涂上相应的颜色。

70

Unit 6 Shopping

A. Let's talk Let's play

夯实基础

一、找出每组单词中不同类的一项，将其序号填入题前括号里。

(   )1. A. small   B. big   C. size
(   )2. A. try   B. shoes   C. hat
(   )3. A. good   B. nice   C. too
(   )4. A. they   B. them   C. I

二、选择正确的答案，将其序号填入题前括号里。

(   )1. —_____
       —Yes, please. I want to buy a coat.
       A. Can I help you?   B. Welcome!   C. Excuse me!

(   )2. These _____ are nice.
       A. shirt   B. shorts   C. skirt

(   )3. Let me try _____.
       A. Size 7   B. 7 size   C. size 7

(   )4. Can I try the red coat _____?
       A. in   B. off   C. on

三、按要求完成下列各题。

1. You can try it on.（改为一般疑问句）

   _____

2. The skirt is too _____.（看图补全句子）

3. These _____ are nice.（看图补全句子）

4. I like this _____. It's _____ _____.
   （看图补全句子）

   size M

5. T-shirt, a, I, buy, to, want (.)（连词成句）

_____

提升能力

四、选择合适的句子补全对话,将其序号填在横线上。(有两项多余)

> A. What colour is the skirt? B. It is just right.
> C. Can I help you? D. Can I try it on?
> E. Here you are. F. Let's try size S.
> G. Let's try size L. H. It is so big!

Assistant（售货员）：Welcome to our shop. 1._____

Nancy：Yes. This pink skirt is nice. 2._____

Assistant：Of course. What size do you wear?

Nancy：Size M, please.

Assistant：OK. 3._____

…

Nancy's mum：Honey, is it OK?

Nancy：Oh, no. 4._____

Nancy's mum：Hmm. 5._____

Nancy：Look! 6._____

A. Let's learn Complete and say

夯实基础

一、选择正确的答案,将其序号填入题前括号里。

(   ) 1. Can I try _____ on?
  A. they B. They C. them

(   ) 2. These gloves _____ nice.
  A. am B. is C. are

( )3. It's hot, so I _____ my jacket.
　　A. take in　　　　B. take off　　　　C. put on

( )4. My _____ is colourful(颜色鲜艳的).
　　A. scarf　　　　B. sunglasses　　　　C. gloves

二、看图，完成下面的句子。

1. Put on your _____, please.

2. It's snowy. Put on your _____.

3. It's sunny. Put on your _____.

4. It's rainy. Take your _____.

提升能力

三、阅读短文，判断下列句子正误，正确的写"T"，错误的写"F"。

　　There are four seasons in a year. In spring(春天), it's warm and sunny. I can wear a blouse and pants. In summer(夏天), it's very hot. I can wear my T-shirt, skirt and sunglasses. And in autumn(秋天), it is cool. I can wear my jacket, sweater and jeans. In winter(冬天), it is very cold. I can wear my hat, scarf, sweater and coat. I love winter best because I can make a snowman in winter.

( )1. It is cool and sunny in spring.

( )2. I can wear my scarf in summer.

( )3. In autumn, it is cold.

( )4. I can't wear my shorts in winter.

( )5. I like summer best.

( )6. I can make a snowman in winter.

A. Let's spell

夯实基础

一、听录音，补全单词。

I have some c_ _ds about animals.
Look at the tig_ _. It is big.
Look at the b_ _d. It is cute.
I can see a h_ _se. It runs fast.
I can see a t_ _tle. It walks slowly.
Look! The eag_ _ has big wings.
I like them all. How about you?

注意 er/le/ur/ar/ir/or 在单词中的发音哟！

二、判断下列每组单词画线部分的发音是否相同，相同的在括号里打"√"，不相同的打"×"。

( ) 1. c<u>ar</u>d   p<u>ar</u>k   ( ) 2. wat<u>er</u>   und<u>er</u>
( ) 3. w<u>or</u>k   m<u>ar</u>k   ( ) 4. g<u>ir</u>l   t<u>ur</u>n

提升能力

三、看图，完成下面的句子。

1. My _____（叔叔）is a cook.

2. My aunt is a _____. She works in the fields(田地).

3. The giraffe is very _____.

4. A cute little girl is playing with a _____.

Unit 6 阶段复习

听力部分

一、听录音,选择你所听到的单词,将其序号填入题前括号里。

(   )1. A. gloves   B. scarf   (   )2. A. shirt   B. T-shirt

(   )3. A. socks   B. shoes   (   )4. A. size   B. sale

(   )5. A. sunglasses   B. umbrella

二、听录音,选择与你所听到的内容相符的图片,将其序号填入题前括号里。

三、听录音,选择正确的答语,将其序号填入题前括号里。

(   )1. A. Good.   B. Here you are.   C. Yes. Can I try it on?

(   )2. A. No. They're too small.   B. No, you can't.

     C. I'm good.

(   )3. A. Oh, they're too big!

     B. Of course. Here you are.

     C. They're just right.

四、听对话,判断下列句子正误,正确的在括号里写"T",错误的写"F"。

(   )1. Amy and her mum are at a clothes shop.

(   )2. Amy wants to try the skirt.

(   )3. Amy can wear the dress in size M.

读写部分

五、选择与每组单词同类的一项,将其序号填入题前括号里。

A. beside   B. cold   C. small   D. gloves   E. these

( )1. big   long   short   ( )2. scarf   sweater   hat

( )3. this   that   those   ( )4. in   on   under

( )5. cool   hot   warm

六、看图,完成下面的句子。

1. Your _____ are cool.

2. I like this yellow _____.

3. Look! The boy's pants are too _____.

4. I want to buy this cute _____.

七、选择正确的答案,将其序号填入题前括号里。

( )1. —_____   —Yes. I want four apples.

    A. Can I help you?   B. Are these your apples?
    C. What colour are they?

( )2. —Can I try the pants on?   —_____

    A. They're just right!   B. Sure. Here you are.
    C. These pants are nice.

( )3. —Are they OK?   —_____

    A. Yes, it is.   B. No, it isn't.   C. No. They are too long.

八、连词成句。

1. gloves, These, nice, are   (.)

2. big, are, They, too （!）

_____

3. put, my, I, on, T-shirt （.）

_____

4. are, They, right, just （!）

_____

九、给下列句子排序,将其序号写在横线上。

A. Of course. Here you are.

B. They are too small. Let me try size 7.

C. Can I help you?

D. Yes. Can I try these on? Size 6, please.

E. Oh, they are just right.

F. They are size 7. Here you are.

正确顺序：_____ _____ _____ A _____ _____ _____

十、任务型阅读。

Sam: It's cool in Beijing. I wear my shirt and pants.

Jim: It's hot in Hong Kong. I wear my T-shirt and shorts.

Mike: It's cold in Harbin. I wear my coat and sweater.

任务一：将下列城市与对应的天气、着装连线。

1. Beijing   2. Hong Kong   3. Harbin

A.   B.   C.

a.   b.   c.

任务二：仿照上面的句子,写一写。

It's _____ in _____. I wear my _____ and _____.

B. Let's talk Let's act

夯实基础

一、选择可以替换句子中画线部分的选项,将其序号填入题前括号里。

( )1. How much are these <u>gloves</u>?
  A. shirt   B. sock   C. shorts

( )2. This skirt is so <u>pretty</u>.
  A. cute   B. like   C. purple

( )3. It is very <u>cheap</u>.
  A. much   B. many   C. expensive

( )4. They're <u>¥40</u>.
  A. fifty yuan   B. fifty yuans   C. forty dollar

二、判断下列对话与图片是否相符,相符的在括号里打"√",不相符的打"×"。

( )1. —How do you like this scarf?
  —It's beautiful.

( )2. —How much is this hat?
  —It's twenty yuan.

( )3. —How do you like those shoes?
  —They are too expensive.

( )4. —How much is this clock?
  —It's sixteen yuan.

三、根据问句选择正确的答语,将其序号填入题前括号里。

( )1. How do you like this T-shirt?   A. It's twenty yuan.
( )2. How much is this skirt?   B. Yes. Can I have a look at this hat?
( )3. Can I help you?   C. They're seventeen yuan.
( )4. How much are these gloves?   D. It is pretty.

Unit 6

提升能力

四、根据图文内容选择正确的选项组合,写在横线上。

It will be hot soon. Linda wants to buy some things to wear on hot days. She has fifty dollars. Choose the things she can buy according to（根据）the prices.

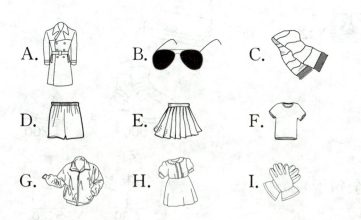

coat……$30
sunglasses……$35
scarf……$12
shorts……$14
skirt……$30
T-shirt……$21
jacket……$25
dress……$38
gloves……$18

Your answer：_____

B. Let's learn Let's play

夯实基础

一、选择合适的选项补全单词。

(　　)1. p__ __tty　　　A. ar　　　B. er　　　C. re

(　　)2. ch__ __p　　　A. oe　　　B. ea　　　C. ae

(　　)3. n__c__　　　　A. i; e　　　B. o; e　　　C. e; e

(　　)4. expens__ __e　A. vi　　　B. if　　　C. iv

二、根据对话内容选择相应的图片,将其序号填入题前括号里。

(　　)1. —How much is that table?

　　　　　—_____.

　　　　　—It's expensive.

A.  $76　　B.  $282　　C.  $64

( )2. —How much is your jacket?
—_____.
—It's cheap.

A. ¥117   B. ¥125   C. ¥35

( )3. —How much is your pencil box? —It's twelve yuan.

A. ¥13   B. ¥12   C. ¥7

三、按要求完成下列各题。

1. The big shoes are _____. （看图补全句子）

   $500   vs $200

2. The shirt is _____. （看图补全句子）

   $30   vs $120

3. It's 15 yuan. （对画线部分提问）
   _____

4. skirt, like, How, this, you, do （?）（连词成句）
   _____

提升能力

四、为下列人物找到他们的物品，连线并依照例子在横线上写出物品的价格。

I have four friends. They are Zhang Peng, Wu Yifan, Sarah and Chen Jie. Look! Zhang Peng has a nice schoolbag. It's yellow. It's forty yuan. Wu Yifan has a blue umbrella. It's expensive. It's one hundred（百） yuan. Sarah has a pretty dress. It's fifty yuan. Chen Jie has a cheap scarf. It's twenty yuan.

1.   2.   3.   4.

A. (dress)   B. (schoolbag)   C. (scarf)   D. (umbrella)

例：¥50

B. Read and write-Let's sing

Unit 6

 夯实基础

一、为下列对话选择合适的图片，将其序号填入题前括号里。

(   )1. —How much is this pretty scarf?
　　　—It's 15 yuan.
　　　—Oh, that's very cheap!

A.

(   )2. —Can I help you?
　　　—Yes, please. Can I try these glasses on?
　　　—Sure. Here you are.

B.

(   )3. —How much are these gloves?
　　　—They are 25 yuan.
　　　—Can I try them on?
　　　—Sure.

C.
￥15

(   )4. —Are the shoes OK?
　　　—No. My feet hurt(疼痛). They are too small.

D.

二、仿照例子写句子。

例：They are very expensive.　　　　　　　　（expensive）
￥500

1._____　　（cheap）
￥32

例：They are too small.　　　　　　　　　　（too small）

2._____　　（too long）

提升能力

三、阅读图片信息,完成下列各题。

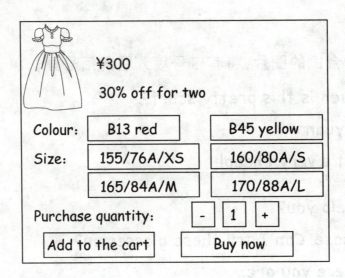

( ) 1. Choose a title for this picture.

　　　A. Shopping in the Clothes Shop

　　　B. Shopping Online

2. This dress has _____ colours.

3. Mary is 160 cm. She can buy size _____.

4. Mary's mum wants to buy two dresses for her two daughters. How much should she pay(付款)? _____.

5. Did you buy things in this way? What did you buy? How much did you pay?

（根据你的实际情况回答）

_____

四、读绘本故事,完成下列任务。

任务一：阅读绘本，从方框中选择合适的选项，将其序号填在横线上。

> A. T-shirt　　B. 99 yuan　　C. 20 yuan
> D. expensive　　E. skirt

任务二：根据绘本故事，判断下列句子正误，正确的写"T"，错误的写"F"。

(　　)1. The skirt is 20 yuan. It's cheap.

(　　)2. The little mouse buys a T-shirt for his mother.

C. Story time

选择合适的单词补全句子，将其序号填在横线上。

> A. dollars　　B. problem　　C. It's
> D. job　　　　E. pretty　　　F. fired

1. Do a good _____.

2. No _____!

3. It's _____, isn't it?

4. _____ cheap, too.

5. Sixteen _____!

6. Zoom, you're _____!

Unit 6 听力训练

一、听录音,选择你所听到的单词,将其序号填入题前括号里。

( ) 1. A. shirt   B. skirt   C. shorts

( ) 2. A. cheap   B. sheep   C. expensive

( ) 3. A. scarf   B. glove   C. love

( ) 4. A. many   B. much   C. some

( ) 5. A. nice   B. rice   C. size

二、听录音,选择与你所听到的内容相符的图片,将其序号填入题前括号里。

( ) 1. A.  B.   ( ) 2. A. B.

( ) 3. A.  B.   ( ) 4. A. B.

三、听录音,选择正确的答语,将其序号填入题前括号里。

( ) 1. A. Yes. I want to buy a book.   B. This book is good.

( ) 2. A. Goodbye.   B. Sure. Here you are.

( ) 3. A. Yes, it is.   B. No. They are too big.

( ) 4. A. Size 9.   B. It's 9 yuan.

( ) 5. A. Yes, you can.   B. No, you don't.

四、听短文,将人物与物品连线,并在相应的横线上写出价格。(写阿拉伯数字)

1. Me   2. Sister   3. Mother   4. Father

A.    B.    C.   D.

¥_____   ¥_____   ¥_____   ¥_____

四、听对话,选择正确的答案,将其序号填入题前括号里。(8%)

( )1. Abby is in the _____ now.
  A. classroom   B. teachers' office   C. gym

( )2. The gym is on the _____ floor.
  A. first   B. second   C. one

( )3. The ground floor in _____ is the first floor in _____.
  A. the USA; the UK   B. the UK; the USA
  C. the UK; China

( )4. _____ is in the teachers' office.
  A. Miss White   B. Miss Green   C. Miss Brown

Writing Part (60%)

五、选择正确的答案,将其序号填入题前括号里。(12%)

( )1. Welcome _____ our library.
  A. to   B. in   C. for

( )2. It's the _____ office.
  A. teachers   B. teachers'   C. teacher is

( )3. We can draw pictures in the _____ room.
  A. music   B. computer   C. art

( )4. Let's play football on the _____.
  A. playground   B. garden   C. gym

( )5. —Is that the computer room?
  —_____
  A. Yes, it does.   B. Yes, we do.   C. No, it isn't.

( )6. —Let's go to the gym.
  —OK. _____
  A. How beautiful!   B. This way, please.   C. Thanks.

六、看图，从方框中选择合适的内容补全句子。(有一项多余)(15%)

```
library        teachers' office    computer room
second floor   music room          playground
```

1. The _____ is on the first floor.

2. We have a _____ in our school.

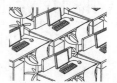

3. —Where is the music room?
   —It's on the _____.

4. —Do you have a _____?
   —Yes, we do.

5. Let's go to the _____ and play football.

七、选择合适的句子补全对话，将其序号填在横线上。(10%)

(It's the School Open Day.)

Sarah: 1._____ This is my classroom.
        That is the teachers' office.
Visitor: 2._____
Sarah: Forty-eight.
Visitor: 3._____
Sarah: Yes. We have many books in it.
Visitor: 4._____
Sarah: Yes. The lunch room is on
        the first floor. 5._____

A. Do you have lunch at school?
B. How many students are there in your class?
C. This way, please.
D. Welcome to my school!
E. Do you have a library?

( )2. A. It's time for PE class.　　B. I like maths class.　　C. It's 3:25.

( )3. A. Excuse me.　　B. Time to go home, kids.　　C. OK.

( )4. A. It's time to get up.　　B. It's time for lunch.

　　　C. It's time to go to bed.

( )5. A. Hurry up! Let's go!

　　　B. No, thank you.

　　　C. Let's go to the playground.

四、听短文，将各个时间与相应的活动连线。(10%)

1.　　2.　　3.　　4.　　5.

A.　　B.　　C.　　D.　　E.

Writing Part(60%)

五、判断下列每组单词画线部分的发音是否相同，相同的打"√"，不相同的打"×"。(8%)

( )1. h<u>a</u>mburger　　S<u>a</u>turday　　( )2. n<u>ur</u>se　　g<u>ir</u>l

( )3. thi<u>r</u>ty　　fo<u>r</u>ty　　( )4. d<u>ir</u>t　　b<u>ir</u>d

六、选择正确的答案，将其序号填入题前括号里。(10%)

( )1. Let's _____ to the classroom!

　　A. go　　B. to go　　C. go to

(　　)2. —It's 8:10 now. —Oh! I'm _____ school.

　　　　A. late　　　　　B. late for　　　　C. late on

(　　)3. It's _____ o'clock. It's time for lunch.

　　　　A. seven　　　　B. six　　　　　　C. twelve

(　　)4. It's time _____ go to bed.

　　　　A. to　　　　　　B. at　　　　　　　C. for

(　　)5. I have a computer class _____ 10:00 _____ the morning.

　　　　A. at; on　　　　B. on; in　　　　　C. at; in

七、选择合适的句子补全对话，将其序号填在横线上。(8%)

Qingqing: 1. _____

Mike: It's three o'clock.

Qingqing: Oh, it's time for music class. Where is the music room?

Mike: 2. _____

Qingqing: OK! 3. _____

Mike: Do you know what next class is?

Qingqing: 4. _____

A. It is on the first floor.

B. It's English class.

C. What time is it?

D. Let's go.

八、看图，完成下面的对话。(12%)

1. Tom: What time is it in Sydney?

　Amy: _____

四、听对话,根据你所听到的内容填写单词完成句子。(10%)

1. It is _____ in Beijing today.

2. It is _____ in Urumqi today.

3. It is _____ in Lhasa today.

4. In Harbin, it is _____ today.

5. It's a nice day in Shanghai today. It is _____.

Writing Part(60%)

五、选择每组单词中不同类的一项,将其序号填入题前括号里。(12%)

( ) 1. A. how   B. fly   C. what

( ) 2. A. Sydney   B. Beijing   C. great

( ) 3. A. swim   B. hot   C. warm

( ) 4. A. sunny   B. kite   C. windy

( ) 5. A. cold   B. cool   C. come

( ) 6. A. snow   B. snowy   C. rainy

六、为下列句子选择合适的图片,将其序号填入题前括号里。(8%)

A. −1℃   B. 20℃   C. 37℃   D. 16℃

( ) 1. It's too hot today. I want to drink more(更多的) water.

( ) 2. It's cool and windy today. Let's fly a kite.

( ) 3. Let's make a snowman. Wow, it's really cold!

( ) 4. It's warm and cloudy! The puppy wants to play with the ball outside.

七、选择正确的答案,将其序号填入题前括号里。(10%)

( ) 1. It's cold _____ Luoyang.

    A. in   B. of   C. on

(　　)2.　—Can I go outside now?

　　　　—No, you _____.

　　　　A. isn't　　　　　　B. don't　　　　　　C. can't

(　　)3.　—What's the weather _____ today?

　　　　—It's cool. We can go to the playground and play football.

　　　　A. for　　　　　　　B. like　　　　　　　C. in

(　　)4.　—Can you _____ your kite?

　　　　—Yes, I can.

　　　　A. play　　　　　　B. go　　　　　　　　C. fly

(　　)5.　It will _____ hot in Sanya tomorrow.

　　　　A. is　　　　　　　B. be　　　　　　　　C. are

八、选择合适的句子补全对话，将其序号填在横线上。(10%)

> A. It's sunny and hot here.
> B. What's the weather like there?
> C. Yes, I can.
> D. Where are you now?
> E. How about Sanya?

Lisa：Hi, Cindy. This is Lisa.

Cindy：Hi, Lisa. 1._____

Lisa：I'm in Beijing.

Cindy：2._____

Lisa：It's snowy and cold in Beijing now. 3._____

Cindy：4._____ I can swim in the sea. Can you play outside?

Lisa：5._____ Haha... I can go skating or make a snowman.

九、看图，完成下面的对话。(6%)

1.　—_____

　　—Yes, it is.

(　　)3. A. It's 4 o'clock.　　　B. There are four.　　　C. I see four.

(　　)4. A. Thank you.　　　B. Hurry up.　　　C. There are sixteen.

(　　)5. A. It's here.　　　B. It's rainy and cool.　　　C. No, it isn't.

四、听短文,判断下列句子正误,正确的写"T",错误的写"F"。(8%)

(　　)1. It's windy and cool in London today.

(　　)2. Susan has breakfast at 7:00.

(　　)3. Susan's classroom is on the first floor.

(　　)4. Susan has a PE class at 9:30 and an English class at 10:30.

Writing Part(60%)

五、选择每组单词中画线部分发音不同的一项,将其序号填入题前括号里。(12%)

(　　)1. A. girl　　　B. bird　　　C. dinner

(　　)2. A. arm　　　B. card　　　C. warm

(　　)3. A. tail　　　B. ball　　　C. wall

(　　)4. A. nurse　　　B. far　　　C. car

(　　)5. A. eraser　　　B. water　　　C. tiger

(　　)6. A. computer　　　B. hamburger　　　C. weather

六、看图,在横线上写出适当的单词或短语,补全句子。(10%)

1. This is the _____.　　　2. It's time for _____.

3. It's time to have _____.　　　4. It's _____ in Kunming.

5. It's _____ in Jilin.

七、选择正确的答案,将其序号填入题前括号里。(10%)

(   )1. Go to the _____. Say hello.
　　　A. teachers' office   B. playground   C. garden

(   )2. Put on your hat. It's _____ today.
　　　A. warm   B. hot   C. cold

(   )3. I have _____ umbrella!
　　　A. not   B. no   C. /

(   )4. Can I have _____ soup?
　　　A. a   B. some   C. an

(   )5. —_____ books are there on your desk?
　　　—Six.
　　　A. How old   B. How much   C. How many

八、看图,选择合适的句子补全对话,将其序号填在横线上。(12%)

(At Sally's home,Xi'an...)

Sally：Zina, come here! This is my birthday gift.

Zina：Cool! A mobile phone(手机)! This afternoon we will have a PE class. Let's check(查询) the weather on the phone!

Sally：OK! 1._____

Zina：Emm... At 4 p.m. What's the weather like then?

Sally：Oh, no. 2._____

Zina：3._____

Sally：Don't worry(别担心)! 4._____

Zina：Yes, you're right. Well, my father is in Sanya now. 5._____

(   )4. The tomatoes are red and round.

(   )5. Jack likes to eat vegetables.

Writing Part(60%)

五、看图,从方框中选择正确的单词完成句子。(8%)

> forks   homework   horse   world

1. I am doing my _____.
2. My father is reading a _____ map.
3. My little brother is playing with a toy _____.
4. My mother is putting _____ and knives on the table.

六、圈出表示蔬菜和农场动物的单词。(7%)

| carrot | garden | sheep | giraffe | milk | banana | potato | lion |
| pear | tomato | cow | farm | hen | water | onion | apple |

七、选择正确的答案,将其序号填入题前括号里。(12%)

(   )1. My grandma has six _____.

    A. sheep   B. sheeps   C. sheepes

(   )2. These _____ green beans.

    A. am   B. is   C. are

(   )3. The cow says "_____."

    A. Meow, meow   B. Quack, quack   C. Moo, moo

(   )4. Are _____ carrots?

    A. these   B. this   C. that

(   )5. —How many _____ do you have?

    —I have six.

    A. horse   B. cow   C. dogs

(　　)6. —_____

—Yes, they are.

    A. Are they cats?　　　　　　B. Is this a duck?

    C. What are those?

八、选择合适的句子补全对话，将其序号填在横线上。(5%)

Amy: Hi, Mike. 1. _____

Mike: Thank you. Wow! The farm is so big! 2. _____

Amy: They are green beans.

Mike: Oh! 3. _____

Amy: No. They are goats.

Mike: 4. _____

Amy: Yes. They are docile(温驯的).

Mike: 5. _____

Amy: Twenty-six.

A. Are these sheep?
B. Do you like goats?
C. Welcome to my grandpa's farm.
D. How many goats are there?
E. What are these?

九、看图，完成下面的句子。(4%)

1. These _____.

2. Those _____.

(   )5. A. Yes, it's John's.   B. Yes, they are.   C. No, it isn't.

四、听对话,判断下列句子正误,正确的写"T",错误的写"F"。(12%)

(   )1. The shirt is Mike's.

(   )2. The green coat is Jim's.

(   )3. The blue shorts are Sam's.

(   )4. The black shorts are Zhang Peng's.

Writing Part(60%)

五、判断每组单词画线部分的发音是否相同,相同的写"T",不相同的写"F"。(12%)

(   )1. peop<u>le</u>   litt<u>le</u>   (   )2. tab<u>le</u>   sma<u>ll</u>   (   )3. unc<u>le</u>   app<u>le</u>

(   )4. <u>le</u>g   midd<u>le</u>   (   )5. bott<u>le</u>   purp<u>le</u>   (   )6. vegetab<u>le</u>   nood<u>le</u>s

六、看图,并根据字母或字母组合提示补全单词,完成对话。(10%)

FOR BOYS   FOR GIRLS

Mum: This is the picture of Daniel's school uniform. The 1. p_____ are

for boys, and the 2. s_____ is for girls.

Dad: Good! Both the boys and girls can wear the 3. s_____. It is made

of wool. And the 4. c_____ is made of wool, too.

Daniel: What is wool?

Mum: It is the soft hair of sheep. Let's say thanks to sheep.

Daniel: Thank you, 5. sh_____.

七、看图,回答下列问题。(9%)

1. Is this hat Lily's?

   _____

2. Whose coat is it?

   _____

3. What colour are these clothes?

   _____

棕色的

Lucy's clothes

八、选择合适的句子补全对话,将其序号填在横线上。(有一项多余)(10%)

Sarah: I can't find my skirt, Mum. 1. _____

Mum: 2. _____

Sarah: It's pink.

Mum: Is this skirt yours?

Sarah: 3. _____ Thanks, Mum!

Mum: But whose shorts are those?

Sarah: 4. _____

Mum: What about this hat? Is this Sam's, too?

Sarah: 5. _____

Mum: Well, put away your clothes, please.

Sarah & Sam: OK, Mum.

A. What colour is it?	B. They are Sam's.
C. Yes, it is.	D. No, they aren't.
E. Where is my skirt?	F. No. It's mine.

九、任务型阅读。(19%)

Dear Mike,

　　This is my first year in China. And I enjoy my first Chinese New Year—the Spring Festival. Look at this picture. They are my Chinese neighbours(邻

Writing Part(60％)

五、判断下列每组单词画线部分的读音是否相同，相同的打"√"，不相同的打"×"。(4％)

(　　)1. g<u>ir</u>l　　　c<u>ar</u>d　　　(　　)2. comput<u>er</u>　　　dinn<u>er</u>

(　　)3. peo<u>pl</u>e　　　ap<u>pl</u>e　　　(　　)4. w<u>or</u>k　　　f<u>or</u>k

六、看图，补全单词。(8％)

1. s_ngla__es

2. gl__es

3. __mb__lla

4. sc__f

七、选择正确的单词补全句子或对话。(10％)

1. She _____(have/has) a pretty hat. I _____(like/likes) its colour.

2. _____(This/These) shoes are cool. Can I try _____(they/them) on?

3. —_____(What/How) do you like it?

　—It's nice.

4. It is cold outside. I want to wear my _____(shirt/coat).

5. It is two _____(yuan/dollar). I _____(will/is) take it.

八、为下列问句选择合适的答语，将其序号填入题前括号里。(10％)

(　　)1. How much is your schoolbag?

(　　)2. How do you like this umbrella?

(　　)3. Can I help you?

(　　)4. Can I try the scarf on?

(　　)5. How much are those big shoes?

A. Yes. I want to buy a notebook.
B. It's seventy-six yuan.
C. They're seventy-six yuan.
D. Sorry, it's not for sale.
E. It's pretty.

九、按要求完成下列各题。(8%)

1. This skirt is expensive.（改为一般疑问句）

    _____ this _____ expensive?

2. This hat is <u>very cool</u>.（对画线部分提问）

    _____ do you _____ this hat?

3. Is the scarf cheap?（看图回答问题） ¥12

    _____

4. What size is your sweater?（看图回答问题） size L

    _____

十、读对话，选出 Pingping 购买的物品，在相应的括号里打"√"，并写出总价。(写阿拉伯数字)(8%)

Shop assistant：Can I help you?

Pingping：Yes. I want to buy a white dress.

Shop assistant：You can try this one on. It is half price today. It's only ninety-eight yuan.

Pingping：Wow! It's very beautiful. I'll take it. These shoes are nice. Can I try them on? Size 5, please.

Shop assistant：Sorry, shoes in size 5 are sold out.

Pingping：Oh, it doesn't matter. This umbrella is nice. How much is it?

Shop assistant：It's eighty-eight yuan.

Pingping：It's too expensive.

Shop assistant：You can take this one. It's only fifty yuan.

Pingping：It's nice. I'll take it.

Shop assistant：OK!

Pingping：Can I try that blue hat on?

Shop assistant：Of course. Here you are.

四、听短文,判断下列句子正误,正确的写"T",错误的写"F"。(10%)

(   )1. Tomorrow is Monday.

(   )2. It's sunny and hot today.

(   )3. Lily goes shopping with her friend.

(   )4. The jacket is 60 yuan.

(   )5. The clothes are nice, but they're not cheap.

Writing Part(60%)

五、判断下列每组单词画线部分的发音是否相同,相同的在括号里打"√",不相同的打"×"。(5%)

(   )1. uncle   noodle   (   )2. fork   world   (   )3. nurse   skirt

(   )4. park   turn   (   )5. ruler   bird

六、给下列单词或短语分类,将其序号填在相应的房子里。(10%)

> A. hen   B. skirt   C. carrot   D. PE class
> E. rainy   F. tomato   G. horse   H. sweater
> I. cloudy   J. music class

1. vegetable   2. animal   3. clothes

4. weather   5. class

七、选择正确的答案,将其序号填入题前括号里。(10%)

(   )1. My classroom is on the _____ floor.

　　A. seven   B. six   C. second

(   )2. It's time _____ go to bed.

　　A. in   B. to   C. for

( )3. School is _____. Let's go home.
   A. up   B. over   C. ready

( )4. _____ your jacket. It's cold.
   A. Put on   B. Take off   C. Put away

( )5. Are _____ your jeans?
   A. it   B. them   C. these

八、看图，完成下面的对话。(10%)

1. —_____?
   —It's _____ o'clock.

2. —What's the weather like today? Is it _____?
   —Yes, it is.

3. —How much is the _____?
   —Sorry, it's not for sale.

4. —Are these _____?
   —Yes, they are.

5. —Is that a shirt?
   —_____.

九、选择合适的句子补全对话，将其序号填在横线上。(有一项多余)(10%)

Amy：1. _____
Mum：It's 7:00. 2. _____
Amy：OK! 3. _____
Mum：It's on the bed.
Amy：No. It's not mine. 4. _____
Mum：5. _____
Amy：It's yellow.
Mum：Oh, it's near the window.

A. It's my sister's.
B. What colour is your sweater?
C. Mum, where is my sweater?
D. It's time to get up.
E. Mum, what time is it?
F. It's time to go to bed.

(   )3. A. Yes, it is.　　　　　B. Yes, we do.　　　　C. It's on the second floor.
(   )4. A. I'm ready.　　　　　B. It's seven o'clock.　C. Let's have breakfast.
(   )5. A. It's beautiful.　　　　B. I like Hangzhou.　　C. It's sunny and hot.

四、听对话,判断下列句子正误,正确的打"√",错误的打"×"。(10%)

(   )1. Danny is at school.
(   )2. The teachers' office is next to Danny's classroom.
(   )3. The art room is on the second floor.
(   )4. Danny likes art class, computer class and PE class.
(   )5. Danny goes to school at six o'clock.

Writing Part(60%)

五、读一读,判断下列句子中单词画线部分的发音是否相同,相同的写"S",不同的写"D"。(6%)

(   )1. The fork and the ball are Mike's.　　(   )2. The horse can work.
(   )3. The bird is hurt.　　　　　　　　　(   )4. Let's go and buy some new socks.
(   )5. Our library is so nice.　　　　　　　(   )6. Put your leg under the table.

六、读一读,找出每组单词或短语中不同类的一项,将其序号填入题前括号里。(6%)

(   )1. A. pretty　　　B. nice　　　　C. expensive　　　D. dress
(   )2. A. music　　　B. English　　　C. breakfast　　　D. art
(   )3. A. carrots　　　B. sheep　　　C. green beans　　D. onions
(   )4. A. cheap　　　B. pants　　　C. coat　　　　　D. socks
(   )5. A. sunny　　　B. cool　　　　C. weather　　　　D. warm
(   )6. A. library　　　B. computer　　C. playground　　D. art room

七、选择正确的答案,将其序号填入题前括号里。(12%)

(   )1. —Amy, it's time to _____. —OK. Goodbye.
　　　　A. get up　　　　B. eat breakfast　　　　C. go home
(   )2. —Let's go to the _____ and play football. —OK.
　　　　A. teachers' office　B. playground　　　　C. library

(   )3. —It's cold in Beijing now. What's the weather like in Sydney?
   —It's _____.
   A. cold   B. hot   C. snowy

(   )4. —A lot of _____! What are those? —They're goats.
   A. animals   B. fruit   C. vegetables

(   )5. —Mum, can I wear my new sweater today? —_____ It's hot.
   A. Yes, you can.   B. No, you can't. C. No, you aren't.

(   )6. —Whose sunglasses are these? —_____
   A. It's mine.   B. They are white. C. They are Zoom's.

八、读一读，根据图意选择合适的单词，模仿范例写句子，注意把句子写完整。(6%)

five   playground   rainy

Is it sunny?
No, it isn't.

1. _____
Yes, it is.

It's ten o'clock.

2. _____

That is the library.

3. _____

九、读一读，选择合适的句子补全对话，将其序号填在横线上。(10%)

Salesperson: 1. _____
Lily's mum: Yes. These shoes are nice. 2. _____
Salesperson: They're ninety-eight yuan.
Lily's mum: 3. _____
Lily: They are very pretty. 4. _____

A. How do you like the shoes?
B. Can I try them on?
C. Can I help you?
D. How much are they?
E. Are they OK?

参考答案

next to Classroom 1.

W：Thank you!

M：You're welcome.

【参考答案】

一、1. A 2. A 3. B 4. B 5. A

二、5 3 1 4 2

三、1. ✕ 2. ✓ 3. ✓ 4. ✕

四、1. B 2. C 3. B 4. A

五、1. C 2. B 3. C 4. A 5. A

六、1. B 2. C 3. A 4. A

七、1. D B E 2. C F A

八、1. school 2. library

　　3. teachers' office

　　4. first floor

　　5. playground

B Let's talk Let's play

一、1. D 2. B 3. A 4. C

二、1. B 2. A 3. C 4. B 5. A

三、1. Forty-one students.

　　2. It is on the second floor.

　　3. Yes，we do.

　　4. No，it isn't.（It is the teachers' office.）

B Let's learn Look，ask and answer

一、1. D 2. C 3. A 4. B

二、1. A 2. B 3. A 4. B

三、1. ✕ 2. ✓ 3. ✓

四、1. Yes；we do   2. second

3. Is that the computer room?

B Read and write-Let's sing

一、

| Library | Computer Room | Classroom 2 | Art Room |
| Classroom 1 | Music Room | Teachers' Office | Gym |

二、1. This is the <u>computer room</u>.

　　2. That is the <u>teachers' office</u>.

　　3. This is the library.

　　4. That is the playground.

三、任务一：tiger rooster singer

　　任务二：1. tiger 2. dancer 3. rooster

　　　　　　4. flower

　　任务三：略

C Story time

一、1. B 2. A 3. C 4. B

二、1. C 2. E；A 3. 略

Unit 1 听力训练

【听力材料】

一、1. sister   2. computer

　　3. number   4. after

　　5. teacher

二、1. W：Where is the teachers' office?

　　　M：It's on the first floor.

　　2. We can draw pictures in the art room.

　　3. W：Is this the computer room?

M：Yes, it is.

4. W：Where are you?

　　M：We are in the library.

5. W：Where is Miss Li?

　　M：She's in the music room.

6. Let's play football on the playground!

三、1. Where's the gym?

2. Is this the library?

3. How many students are there in your class?

4. Do you have a music room?

四、Chen Jie：Welcome to my school, Amy.

　Amy：Your school is nice, Chen Jie! Do you have a library?

　Chen Jie：Yes. The library is on the second floor. We often read books there.

　Amy：Where is the teachers' room?

　Chen Jie：The teachers' room is next to the computer room.

　Amy：Is that the art room?

　Chen Jie：No, it isn't. It's the music room. We sing and dance there.

[参考答案]

一、1. C　2. C　3. B　4. B　5. A

二、6　5　4　2　1　3

三、1. A　2. B　3. A　4. B

四、1. F　2. T　3. F　4. T

Unit 2　What time is it?

A. Let's talk　Let's play

一、1. over　2. to　3. go　4. for

二、1. ×　2. ×　3. √　4. ×　5. √　6. ×

三、1. C　2. B　3. D　4. A

四、1. 14:30　2. time　3. 22:30　4. bed
　5. 6:30　6. get up（第6小题答案不唯一，合理即可）

A. Let's learn　Let's do

一、(1. —B—c)　2. —E—b　3. —A—d
　4. —C—e　5. —D—a

二、1. E　2. F　3. D　4. B　5. C　6. A

三、1. T　2. F　3. F

四、1. It's four o'clock.

2. read; write

3. dinner

4. It's time for English class.

5. Let's eat some rice.

A. Let's spell

[听力材料]

一、Little bird, little bird, what do you see?

　I see a green turtle looking at me.

　Green turtle, green turtle, what do you see?

　I see a purple fish looking at me.

　Purple fish, purple fish, what do you see?

　I see a nice girl looking at me.

[参考答案]

一、bird; bird; turtle; turtle; turtle; purple;
　Purple; purple; girl

二、1. √　2. √　3. ×　4. ×

三、1. hamburger; dinner　2. sister; nurse

3. girl; bird

A. Let's spell

[听力材料]

一、Mr Shark is playing with his ball.

He gets a call from Mr Hall.

There's a party on Mars.

Although it is so far,

he can drive his super car and then dance with Mr Hall.

[参考答案]

一、Shark；ball；call；Hall；party；Mars；far；car；Hall

二、1. tall；wall 2. car；arm

三、1. bar：Mark farmer arms hard art garden farm

2. all：Fall tall small ball mall

大怪物的名字：Mark

小怪物的名字：Fall

Unit 3 阶段复习

[听力材料]

一、1. hot 2. cool 3. warm 4. ball 5. arm

二、1. It's cold outside. Put on your hat.

2. It's warm outside.

3. It's hot outside.

4. It's warm inside. Take off your shoes.

三、1. Can I go outside now?

2. Mum, what time is it?

3. Can I have some soup?

4. Is it hot outside?

5. Is it cold?

四、Good morning. This is the weather report. It's cloudy and warm in Kunming. It's windy and cool in Qingdao. It's sunny and hot in Sanya. It's snowy and cold in Shenyang.

[参考答案]

一、1. A 2. B 3. A 4. B 5. A

二、1. ✗ 2. ✓ 3. ✓ 4. ✗

三、1. B 2. A 3. A 4. B 5. A

四、1. B 2. D 3. C 4. A

五、1. B 2. A 3. A 4. B

六、1. hot 2. cool 3. warm 4. cold

七、1. B 2. C 3. B 4. B

八、1. B 2. C 3. D 4. A

九、任务一：hot；cold

任务二：1. —C 2. —A 3. —B

任务三：1. T 2. F 3. F

B. Let's talk Let's play

一、1. cloudy；warm 2. sunny；hot

3. rainy；cool

二、1. A 2. A 3. C

三、任务一：1. —C 2. —A 3. —D 4. —E 5. —B

任务二：No, she can't.

任务三：略

B. Let's learn Let's play

一、1. F 2. T 3. T 4. F 5. F

二、1. Yes；it is

2. Sydney；hot/sunny；sunny/hot

3. cool/rainy；rainy/cool；Beijing

三、1. C　2. B　3. B　4. C

B　Read and write-Let's sing

一、1. 左图　2. 右图　3. 左图　4. 左图

二、1. sunny/hot；hot/sunny　2. snowy

3. It is cold outside.

4. What is the weather like today?

三、任务一：1. F　2. T　3. F

任务二：1. snowy　2. make a snowman

3. Sydney　4. hot　5. sunny

四、任务一：1. T　2. F

任务二：1. snowball

2. snowmen

3. snow

孩子是开心的表情（画图略）

任务三：A snowy day is good, because children can make snowmen. 或 A snowy day is not good, because the farmer's donkeys get hungry more easily/because the postman has a bad fall and breaks his leg.（答案不唯一）

C　Story time

一、1. B　2. C　3. D　4. A

二、任务一：1. C　2. B

任务二：Yes. Use lots of salt. /Yes. Use a magnet.（答案不唯一）

Unit 3　听力训练

[听力材料]

一、salt　fall　bark　star　card

二、1. What's the weather like in Beijing?

2. Is it warm today?

3. Mum, can I go swimming with Mike?

4. Hi, Lisa! How are you?

5. It's 30 degrees. It's very hot. How about Changsha?

三、Good morning, everyone. This is the world weather report. It's cool and rainy in London. In San Francisco, it's cloudy in the morning, but it's sunny in the afternoon. It's cold and snowy in Sydney. It's hot and sunny in Cairo. Thanks for listening.

[参考答案]

一、

s	g	l	f	a	l	l
j	a	v	x	z	c	s
b	s	l	m	r	e	t
a	q	a	t	u	y	s
r	r	d	l	f	g	t
k	h	j	n	t	m	a
c	a	r	d	z	x	r

二、1. C　2. A　3. B　4. A　5. A

三、1. C G　2. A E　3. B F　4. D E

Unit 4　At the farm

A　Let's talk　Let's play

一、1. B　2. A　3. B　4. A

二、1. B　2. C　3. B　4. A

三、1. B　2. C　3. A

四、1. C　2. B　3. A

A　Let's learn　Let's chant

一、1. green beans　2. carrot　3. tomato

四、1. F 2. F 3. T 4. F 5. T

Unit 5 My clothes

A Let's talk Let's play

一、1. A 2. C 3. B

二、1. √ 2. × 3. √

三、1. they aren't; John's
   2. it isn't; Chen Jie's
   3. Yes, they are

四、1. Whose 2. ape's 3. is 4. giraffe's

A Let's learn Let's do

一、1. dress 2. hat 3. pants 4. skirt

二、1. E 2. D 3. B 4. C 5. A

三、1. that dress; those
   2. I like this skirt; I like these skirts

四、Chen Jie: A Amy: B D Wu Yifan: C

A Let's spell

[听力材料]

一、Twinkle, twinkle, little star.
   Uncle Turtle chants to his son,
   "Little Bee lights a candle.
   Mr Eagle flies in the sky…"

[参考答案]

一、twinkle; little; Uncle; Turtle;
   candle; Eagle

二、1. × 2. × 3. √ 4. √

三、1. table 2. people; little

四、people; Needle; bicycle

Unit 5 阶段复习

[听力材料]

一、1. clothes 2. skirt 3. whose 4. people 5. table

二、1. Hang up your shirt.
   2. Put away your hat.
   3. I like those pants.
   4. It's Amy's skirt.

三、John: Sarah, is this your hat?
   Sarah: No, it isn't. It's Chen Jie's.
   John: Are these blue pants yours?
   Sarah: No, they aren't. My pants are pink. They are Mike's.

四、W: It's time to pack my things. Can you help me, Dad?
   M: Of course.
   W: Where is my dress?
   M: Oh, it's in your bedroom.
   W: Where is my hat?
   M: Is it white?
   W: No. It's pink.
   M: Look! It's in the living room.
   W: Where are my shoes?
   M: What colour are they?
   W: They are black.
   M: They are in the bathroom. Don't forget your skirt. It's in your study.
   W: Thank you so much, Dad.

[参考答案]

一、1. A 2. B 3. A 4. B 5. A

二、1. B 2. A 3. A 4. B

三、1. A 2. C 3. B

四、卧室: A 书房: D

客厅：B 浴室：C

五、1. B 2. C 3. A 4. B 5. A

六、1. A 2. C 3. B 4. A 5. B

七、1. Whose 2. sister's 3. this 4. dress
　　5. Chinese 6. those 7. pants

八、1. D 2. A 3. C

九、任务一：1. —A；蓝色 2. —E；红色
　　　　　　3. —B；绿色 4. —D；黄色
　　　　　　5. —C；粉红色

任务二：略

B. Let's talk Let's find out

一、1. A 2. C 3. B 4. D

二、1. D 2. E 3. A 4. C

三、1. dress；mine
　　2. Whose hat is it?
　　　It's Mike's.
　　3. pants；Tina's
　　4. Whose shoes are these?
　　　They are David's.

B. Let's learn Let's find out

一、1. C 2. A 3. C

二、1. C 2. A 3. B 4. E 5. D
（答案合理即可）

三、1. B 2. A 3. C 4. A

B. Read and write-Let's sing

一、1. C 2. B 3. C 4. C

二、1. These are Amy's socks.
　　2. This is Mike's sweater.

三、任务一：1. B 2. C 3. E 4. A D

任务二：1. T 2. F 3. T 4. F

四、任务一：1. T 2. F

任务二：

	robes made of yak wool	coats	hats	mittens	scarves
Iqaluit			√	√	
The northern area（地区）of Nepal	√		√		√

C. Story time

一、1. C 2. B 3. F 4. D 5. E 6. A

二、1. C 2. B
　　3. She needs shoes, warm clothes and food.
　　（答案不唯一，合理即可）

Unit 5 听力训练

〔听力材料〕

一、e. g. bottle   mottle
　　1. cattle   wattle
　　2. nettle   kettle

二、1. Alice：Mum, where are my football shorts?
　　Alice's mum：They're in your bedroom.

2. Tom：Look at my clothes for the basketball class, Dad.
　　Tom's dad：Cool! A white T-shirt and shorts.

3. Linda's grandma：Linda, hurry up. It's time to go to school.
　　Linda：Grandma, where are my blouse and skirt?

4. Cindy：Mum, I want to wear my new dress.

M：They're Amy's.

2. Oh，the T-shirt is too small for me!

3. M：Sarah，are these shoes yours?

　W：Yes，they are.

　M：They're so nice.

4. M：How do you like this dress?

　W：It's very pretty.

三、1. Can I help you?

2. Can I try it on?

3. Are they OK?

4. What size?

5. It's sunny and hot outside. Can I put on my sunglasses?

四、Today I go shopping with my family. My mother buys a hat for me. It's twenty-eight yuan. She buys a dress for my little sister. It's ninety yuan. Look at the sunglasses. They are my mother's. They are one hundred yuan. Whose shoes are these? They are my father's. They are a little expensive. They are two hundred yuan.

[参考答案]

一、1. C 2. A 3. A 4. B 5. C
二、1. A 2. B 3. A 4. A
三、1. A 2. B 3. B 4. A 5. A
四、1. —A；￥28   2. —D；￥90
　　3. —C；￥100   4. —B；￥200

附录 Ⅱ

评价标准（参考）：

优秀 A≥85%　　　　良好 85%＞B≥70%

合格 70%＞C≥60%　　不合格 D＜60%

核心能力评价（一）

[听力材料]

一、1. floor   2. forty   3. class   4. first
　　5. playground   6. art   7. music
　　8. gym   9. dinner   10. river

二、1. This is the music room. It's on the second floor.

2. This is the art room. It's next to the music room.

3. This is the computer room.

4. This is the library. It's on the first floor.

5. This is the teachers' office.

6. This is my classroom. It's next to the teachers' office.

三、1. Where's the teachers' office?

2. Is that your music room?

3. Do you have a computer room?

4. How many students are there in your class?

5. Let's go to the playground.

四、Kim：Hello，Abby. This is Kim. Where are you now?

Abby：I'm in the gym. It's on the ground floor.

Kim：What? The gym is on the first floor?

Abby：Oh，yes. The ground floor in the UK is the first floor in the USA.

Kim：I see. Miss Brown is waiting for you. She's in the teachers' office. And the office is on the second floor. That's the first floor in the UK.

Abby: OK. Thank you.

〖参考答案〗

一、1. B 2. B 3. A 4. A 5. A 6. B 7. B 8. B 9. A 10. A

二、3 1 2 4 6 5

三、1. A 2. B 3. C 4. A 5. B

四、1. C 2. A 3. B 4. C

五、1. A 2. B 3. C 4. A 5. C 6. B

六、1. teachers' office   2. computer room
  3. second floor   4. library
  5. playground

七、1. D 2. B 3. E 4. A 5. C

八、1. This is the playground.
  2. That is the teachers' office.
  3. Is that your school?

九、任务一：1. D 2. C 3. E 4. A 5. B
  任务二：1. computer room   2. library

核心能力评价（二）

〖听力材料〗

一、1. school   2. breakfast
  3. English   4. now
  5. thirty   6. hamburger
  7. go to school   8. get up

二、1. It's 8:30 now.
  2. Eat some rice.
  3. It's time for bed.
  4. It's 10 o'clock. Time for music class.
  5. It's time for dinner.

6. It's time to go to school.

三、1. Where is Amy?
  2. What time is it?
  3. Let's go to school.
  4. It's 10 p.m. now.
  5. Oh! It's 9 o'clock. Time for English class.

四、Hello, I'm Long Yiming. I'm 10 years old. I get up at 6:30 every day. And then I have breakfast at 6:50. At 10:00, I have an English class. In the afternoon, I have a music class at 2:10. I have dinner at 7 p.m. I go to sleep at 9:20.

〖参考答案〗

一、1. B 2. A 3. B 4. A 5. A 6. A 7. B 8. B

二、1. A 2. B 3. B 4. A 5. B 6. B

三、1. B 2. C 3. C 4. C 5. A

四、1.—B 2.—A 3.—D 4.—E 5.—C

五、1. ✗ 2. ✓ 3. ✗ 4. ✓

六、1. A 2. B 3. C 4. A 5. C

七、1. C 2. A 3. D 4. B

八、1. It's four o'clock.
  2. It's one o'clock.
  3. It's six o'clock.

九、任务一：3 5 4 1 6 2
  任务二：1. F 2. F 3. T 4. F 5. T

核心能力评价（三）

〖听力材料〗

一、1. It's snowy and cold in Xi'an.

十一、任务一：Animal：母鸡 马 奶牛 绵羊

Vegetable：洋葱 土豆 胡萝卜 西红柿

任务二：1. big 2. horses 3. fresh

核心能力评价（五）

[听力材料]

一、1. T-shirt 2. shorts 3. put away

4. I like those socks.

5. Whose sweater is it?

二、1. I have a jacket.

2. Where is my skirt?

3. This dress is Amy's.

4. These are my father's shorts.

三、1. What colour is this coat?

2. What's this?

3. Whose pants are these?

4. Where are the socks?

5. Are these shirts yours?

四、Miss Green：What a mess！Whose coat is this?

Zhang Peng：It's Mike's.

Miss Green：Is this green shirt yours，Zhang Peng?

Zhang Peng：No，it isn't. It's Jim's. Mine is white.

Miss Green：Are these blue shorts yours?

Zhang Peng：No. They're Sam's. Those brown shorts are mine.

[参考答案]

一、1. B 2. C 3. B 4. C 5. A

二、1. B 2. B 3. B 4. A

三、1. A 2. C 3. A 4. A 5. B

四、1. F 2. F 3. T 4. F

五、1. T 2. F 3. T 4. F 5. T 6. T

六、1. pants 2. skirt 3. sweater 4. coat

5. sheep

七、1. No，it isn't. 2. It is Lucy's.

3. They are brown.

八、1. E 2. A 3. C 4. B 5. F

九、任务一：略

任务二：1. T 2. T 3. F 4. F

任务三：略

核心能力评价（六）

[听力材料]

一、1. The sunglasses are nice.

2. The dress is too expensive.

3. The scarf is nice.

4. The skirt is cheap.

5. This is Mike's umbrella.

6. Those gloves are yours.

二、1. The shoes are 138 yuan.

2. The football is 46 yuan.

3. The potatoes are 2 yuan.

4. The jeans are 95 yuan.

三、1. How much is this shirt?

2. Is that dress cheap?

3. How do you like this T-shirt?

4. Can I try the pants on?

5. Where are the sunglasses?

四、Look! Many clothes are on the sofa. The shoes are black. The shorts are nice. The hat is blue. The dress is white. It's pretty. We like them very much.

[参考答案]

一、5 6 1 3 4 2

二、1. 138 2. 46 3. 2 4. 95

三、1. B 2. C 3. A 4. B 5. C

四、1. shoes 2. shorts 3. hat 4. dress 5. pretty

五、1. × 2. √ 3. √ 4. ×

六、1. sunglasses 2. gloves 3. umbrella 4. scarf

七、1. has; like 2. These; them 3. How 4. coat 5. yuan; will

八、1. B 2. E 3. A 4. D 5. C

九、1. Is; skirt
    2. How; like
    3. Yes, it is.
    4. It's size L.

十、帽子、雨伞和连衣裙
    Total：¥166

十一、任务一：1. D 2. E 3. F 4. A 5. C 6. B
    任务二：1. F 2. F 3. T

期末核心能力评价

[听力材料]

一、1. Wash your skirt, Amy.
    2. Whose scarf is this?
    3. Welcome to our school.
    4. Her coat is very cheap.
    5. Dad, can I wear your T-shirt?

二、1. It's snowy today.
    2. Go to the garden. Water the flowers.
    3. Put on your hat.
    4. It's time for PE class. Let's jump and run.
    5. Put away your pants.

三、1. How much are the pants?
    2. Where is my jacket?
    3. What's the weather like in Wuhan?
    4. Whose shirt is this?
    5. Can I try the shoes on?

四、 Today is Sunday. It's sunny and warm. Lily goes shopping with her mum. They buy a pair of shoes, a jacket and a skirt. The shoes are 120 yuan. The jacket is 60 yuan. The skirt is 45 yuan. They're nice and cheap.

[参考答案]

一、1. B 2. B 3. A 4. B 5. B

二、1. √ 2. √ 3. × 4. √ 5. √

三、1. B 2. A 3. C 4. A 5. C

四、1. T 2. F 3. F 4. T 5. F

五、1. √ 2. × 3. √ 4. × 5. ×

六、1. C F 2. A G 3. B H 4. E I 5. D J

七、1. C 2. B 3. B 4. A 5. C

八、1. What time is it; three
    2. sunny

3. computer

4. cows

5. No, it isn't

九、1. E 2. D 3. C 4. A 5. B

十、任务一：1. F 2. T 3. F 4. F 5. T

任务二：1. forks；knives

2. second floor

3. Chongqing

浙江省某市期末核心能力评价

[听力材料]

一、1. short 2. cow 3. five fifteen

4. forty 5. weather 6. those

7. sunny 8. music

二、1. W：What's the weather like today?

M：It's cold.

2. W：What are these?

M：They're potatoes.

3. W：What time is it?

M：It's 12:00. It's time for lunch.

4. W：Is it a skirt?

M：No, it isn't. It's a sweater.

5. W：Where is the teachers' office?

M：It's on the second floor.

6. W：Can I help you?

M：Yes. I want an umbrella, please.

三、1. Whose shoes are they?

2. Do you have a new classroom?

3. Is it cloudy today?

4. What time is it now?

5. How do you like this dress?

四、Mike：Good morning, Danny.

Danny：Welcome to my school, Mike.

Mike：Thank you. Wow! Your school is so big.

Danny：Yes, it is.

Mike：Where is your classroom?

Danny：It's on the second floor. We have an art room. It's next to my classroom.

Mike：Do you have a computer room?

Danny：Yes. It's on the first floor. I like computer class.

Mike：When do you go to school?

Danny：I often go to school at seven o'clock.

Mike：Me, too.

[参考答案]

一、1. C 2. A 3. B 4. C 5. B 6. C 7. A 8. C

二、1. A 2. B 3. A 4. A 5. B 6. B

三、1. C 2. C 3. A 4. B 5. A

四、1. √ 2. × 3. √ 4. × 5. ×

五、1. S 2. D 3. S 4. D 5. S 6. D

六、1. D 2. C 3. B 4. A 5. C 6. B

七、1. C 2. B 3. B 4. A 5. B 6. C

八、1. Is it rainy?

2. It's five o'clock.

3. That is the playground.

九、1. C 2. D 3. A 4. B 5. E

十、1. A 2. A 3. B 4. B 5. B

十一、1. F 2. T 3. F 4. T 5. F

classroom is on the second floor. We have a PE class at nine o'clock. And we have an English class at ten thirty.

[参考答案]

一、1. C 2. C 3. A 4. B 5. A

二、1. B 2. A 3. A 4. A 5. B 6. A

三、1. A 2. B 3. A 4. C 5. B

四、1. T 2. T 3. F 4. F

五、1. C 2. C 3. A 4. A 5. A 6. B

六、1. computer room 2. music class 3. PE class 4. cloudy 5. snowy

七、1. A 2. C 3. B 4. B 5. C

八、1. B 2. E 3. F 4. D 5. A 6. C

九、任务一：1. B 2. C 3. C 4. B 5. A

任务二：1. It's time to go to school.
2. It's time for Chinese class.
3. It's time for PE class.

核心能力评价（四）

[听力材料]

一、1. fork 2. work 3. potato 4. hen 5. these 6. horse

二、1. What are they?
2. How many cows are there?
3. What colour are the carrots?
4. Is it a potato?

三、Mike：I'm Mike. I'd like some chicken and soup, please.

Amy：I'm Amy. I'd like some potatoes and noodles.

Sarah：I'm Sarah. I'd like some carrots and fish.

John：I'm John. I'd like some beef and tomatoes.

Oliver：I'm Oliver. I'd like some green beans and a salad.

四、Hello, I'm Jack. I live on a farm. There are lots of animals and vegetables on the farm. Look! There are some horses. They are running. And there are many sheep over there. I like tomatoes. They are red and round. I like green beans, too. They are long. Vegetables are healthy. I like to eat them.

[参考答案]

一、1. A 2. B 3. A 4. B 5. B 6. B

二、1. B 2. A 3. A 4. A

三、Mike：A I Amy：D F
Sarah：E G John：B C
Oliver：H J

四、1. T 2. F 3. F 4. T 5. T

五、1. homework 2. world 3. horse 4. forks

六、圈出 carrot、sheep、potato、tomato、cow、hen、onion

七、1. A 2. C 3. C 4. A 5. C 6. A

八、1. C 2. E 3. A 4. B 5. D

九、1. are cows 2. are hens

十、5 1 2 4 3

2. Is it sunny and hot in Haikou?

3. It's cloudy in London.

4. It's 13 degrees today. It's cool.

5. Can I have some soup?

二、1. It's snowy today. Let's make a snowman.

2. It's rainy outside.

3. It's warm today.

4. It's sunny and cool in Sydney.

5. It's hot. Let's go swimming.

三、1. Is it cold?

2. What's the weather like in Guangzhou?

3. Can I make a snowman?

4. Is it cool in Changsha?

5. Is it warm in Hefei?

四、W: What's the weather like in Beijing today?

M: It's rainy.

W: How about Urumqi?

M: It is snowy today.

W: What's the weather like in Lhasa?

M: It is cloudy today.

W: Is it a nice day in Harbin?

M: No, it isn't. It is windy. But it's a nice day in Shanghai today. It is sunny.

[参考答案]

一、1. C　2. A　3. B　4. C　5. A

二、1. √　2. √　3. ×　4. ×　5. √

三、1. A　2. C　3. A　4. B　5. A

四、1. rainy　2. snowy　3. cloudy
　　4. windy　5. sunny

五、1. B　2. C　3. A　4. B　5. C　6. A

六、1. C　2. D　3. A　4. B

七、1. A　2. C　3. B　4. C　5. B

八、1. D　2. B　3. E　4. A　5. C

九、1. Is it sunny?　　2. No, it isn't.

3. Is it windy?

十、任务一：1. B　2. A

任务二：1. snowy　2. cold　3. play football
　　　　4. sunny　5. warm

阶段核心能力评价

[听力材料]

一、1. ball　2. farm　3. playground

4. music class　5. Can I go outside now?

二、1. It's time for Chinese class.

2. It's ten twenty-five.

3. Wake up. It's time to get up.

4. It's cold and snowy today.

5. The gym is on the first floor. The art room is on the second floor.

6. It's warm and cloudy in my city.

三、1. Where is your classroom?

2. Do you have a lunch room?

3. What time is it?

4. How many chairs are there?

5. What's the weather like today?

四、　　Hi, I'm Susan. It is windy and cool in London today. I get up at 6:30. I have breakfast at 7:00. Then I go to school. There is a big library on the first floor. My

2. John, are they OK?

3. Can I try these on?

四、Assistant: Can I help you?

Amy: Yes. That dress is nice. Can I try it on?

Cindy's mum：OK. But put on your jacket. It's windy outside.

三、1. Can you help me?

2. Whose white socks are these?

3. Mum，where is my dress?

4. Are they your shorts?

5. Is this yours?

四、David's dad：Oh dear! You have so many clothes! Let's pack them together.

David：OK，Dad! These blue pants are nice. I want to take them.

David's dad：OK. It's cold in Beijing. You should also take this red coat and the yellow sweater.

David：Look! My blue and white jacket! I want to take it，too.

David's dad：All right. We have to go now. Your mum is waiting for us.

【参考答案】

一、1. wattle 2. nettle；kettle

二、1. A 2. B 3. B 4. B

三、1. B 2. C 3. A 4. A 5. C

四、划去短裤和短裙；
夹克衫——蓝白相间；毛衣——黄色；
长裤——蓝色；外套——红色

Unit 6 Shopping

A. Let's talk Let's play

一、1. C 2. A 3. C 4. B

二、1. A 2. B 3. C 4. C

三、1. Can I try it on?

2. big 3. shoes

4. sweater；size M

5. I want to buy a T-shirt.

四、1. C 2. D 3. E 4. H 5. F 6. B

A. Let's learn Complete and say

一、1. C 2. C 3. B 4. A

二、1. gloves 2. scarf 3. sunglasses

4. umbrella

三、1. F 2. F 3. F 4. T 5. F 6. T

A. Let's spell

[听力材料]

一、I have some cards about animals.

Look at the tiger. It is big.

Look at the bird. It is cute.

I can see a horse. It runs fast.

I can see a turtle. It walks slowly.

Look! The eagle has big wings.

I like them all. How about you?

[参考答案]

一、cards；tiger；bird；horse；turtle；eagle

二、1. √ 2. √ 3. × 4. √

三、1. uncle 2. farmer 3. tall 4. ball

Unit 6 阶段复习

[听力材料]

一、1. scarf 2. shirt 3. socks 4. size

5. umbrella

二、1. This is my shirt. It's size M.

2. The shoes are too big.

3. Those are my gloves.

三、1. Can I help you?

B. Let's learn　Draw and say

一、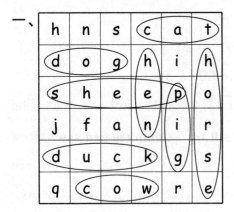

二、1. cows　2. three　3. aren't; ducks

4. They are horses

三、1. They are so cute!

2. How many horses do you have?

3. Are they hens?

4. What are they?

四、1. F　2. F　3. T　4. T　5. F

B. Read and write-Let's sing

一、1. is　2. They　3. sheep　4. has

二、1. √　×　2. √　×　3. √　√

三、1. These are tomatoes.

Those are green beans.

2. 略

四、任务一：1. aren't　2. carrots　3. Rabbit

4. pumpkins　5. carrots

任务二：1. F　2. T　3. F　4. T

C. Story time

一、1. F　2. H　3. D　4. B　5. G　6. A　7. C

8. E

二、任务一：1. Tiger　2. Rabbit　3. Horse

4. Sheep　5. Dog　6. Pig

任务二：圈出 A、D、F、J

任务三：略

Unit 4　听力训练

[听力材料]

一、1. horse　2. cow　3. sheep　4. these

5. potatoes

二、1. M：Are they apples?

W：No. They are tomatoes.

2. W：Are those hens?

M：Yes, they are.

3. W：What are these?

M：They are potatoes.

4. W：Are those horses?

M：No. They are cows.

三、1. Are these sheep?

2. What colour are the onions?

3. What's this?

4. Is this a tomato?

5. What are these?

四、　This is Uncle Andy's farm. There is a vegetable garden. Look! These are potatoes and tomatoes. Those are onions, carrots and green beans. There are many animals, too. These are hens and ducks. Those are cows. There are two horses on the farm, too. I like to ride the horses. I love to play on the farm. It's big and nice.

[参考答案]

一、1. A　2. B　3. A　4. A　5. B

二、1. B　2. A　3. A　4. B

三、1. B　2. A　3. C　4. A　5. B

4. potato

二、1. 圈出 are、long 2. 圈出 carrots、They're

3. 圈出 potatoes 4. 圈出 tomatoes

5. 圈出 onions、me

三、1. × 2. √ 3. ×

四、任务一：1.—D 2.—C 3.—E 4.—A

5.—B

任务二：略

A. Let's spell

[听力材料]

一、1. fork 2. world 3. forty

4. north 5. for 6. homework

[参考答案]

一、1. A 2. A 3. A 4. B 5. A 6. B

二、1. A C D F H 2. B E G

三、1. B 2. D 3. C 4. A

四、1. fork 2. horse 3. homework

Unit 4 阶段复习

[听力材料]

一、1. they 2. carrot

3. What are these?

4. Are these tomatoes?

5. They're so long!

二、1. It's a carrot.

2. It's a tomato.

3. This is a potato.

4. They are green beans.

5. We do our homework.

三、John：What do you like，Chen Jie?

Chen Jie：I like tomatoes.

John：What do you like，Sarah?

Sarah：I like potatoes.

John：What do you like，Wu Yifan?

Wu Yifan：I like carrots.

四、My grandpa has a garden. Look! The tomatoes are red and juicy. The potatoes are big and brown. The green beans are long. And there are also some carrots. Grandpa tells me they are good for my eyes. I like this garden.

[参考答案]

一、1. B 2. A 3. A 4. B 5. C

二、1. × 2. × 3. √ 4. √ 5. √

三、1.—B 2.—C 3.—A

四、1. F 2. F 3. T 4. F 5. T

五、1. B 2. D 3. A 4. C

六、1. C 2. A 3. B 4. C

七、1. tomatoes

2. green beans

3. potatoes

4. Are these carrots?

5. What are these?

八、任务一：A B C E F

任务二：1. Carrots 2. apple

九、任务一：1. B 2. D 3. C 4. A

任务二：1. T 2. F 3. T

B. Let's talk Let's play

一、1. D 2. E 3. F 4. B 5. A 6. C

二、1. B 2. C 3. C

三、3 1 6 4 2 5

四、1. E 2. C 3. B 4. A

三、任务一：1. C 2. H 3. D 4. E 5. B
　　　　　　6. G 7. A 8. F
　　任务二：1. T 2. F 3. T 4. T

C. Story time

一、1. ✕　2. ✓　3. ✓

二、任务一：1. 画3点钟　2. 画9点钟
　　　　　　3. 画1点钟　4. 画8点钟

　　任务二：1. go to bed
　　　　　　2. evening；morning
　　　　　　3. ten o'clock；Tokyo（答案不唯一）

Unit 2　听力训练

〔听力材料〕

一、1. Tom：Mum, I'm hungry.

　　　Mum：Oh! It's eleven forty-five. Let's go and have lunch.

　2. W：What time is it?

　　　M：It's ten o'clock. It's time for music class. Let's go to the music room.

　3. Mum：John, it's six thirty. Time to get up!

　　　John：OK, Mum.

　4. M1：It's five o'clock.

　　　M2：School is over. Let's play football together.

　　　M1：Good idea!

二、1. What time is it?
　　2. Where are you?
　　3. What can you do in the music class?
　　4. Do you like PE class?

三、（Chen Jie is talking with her friends on WeChat.）

　　Chen Jie：Where are you, Amy?
　　Amy：I'm in London.
　　Chen Jie：In Beijing, it's 8 p.m. What time is it there?
　　Amy：It's 12 o'clock.
　　Chen Jie：Where are you, Pedro?
　　Pedro：I'm in Madrid. It's 1 p.m.
　　Chen Jie：Where are you, Oliver?
　　Oliver：I'm in Sydney. It's 10 p.m.
　　Chen Jie：What about you, Mike?
　　Mike：I'm in Toronto. It's 7 a.m. here.

〔参考答案〕

一、1. B 2. A 3. B 4. A

二、1. A 2. B 3. B 4. B

三、1. C d 2. A c 3. D a 4. B b

Unit 3　Weather

A. Let's talk　Let's play

一、1. D 2. C 3. B 4. A

二、1. B 2. C 3. A

三、1. soup；you can
　　2. play football；you can't
　　3. have some milk；Yes, you can

四、任务一：1. D 2. E 3. A 4. F 5. C
　　任务二：1. ✕ 2. ✓ 3. ✕

A. Let's learn　Let's chant

一、1. F 2. F 3. T 4. T

二、1. ✓ 4. ✓

三、1. B 2. A 3. D 4. C

四、1. warm　2. cool　3. cold　4. hot

Unit 2 阶段复习

【听力材料】

一、1. birth 2. hamburger
　　3. thirty 4. lunch
　　5. music class

二、1. It's 9:00. It's time for English class.
　　2. It's 7:00. It's time for dinner.
　　3. Let's eat some rice.

三、1. It's time for PE class.
　　2. What time is it?
　　3. Where is the gym?
　　4. It's time for dinner.

四、Tom: Hello, Amy. Where are you?
　　Amy: Hi, Tom. I'm in Sydney. What time is it in Beijing, Tom?
　　Tom: It's seven o'clock here. What time is it there?
　　Amy: It's nine o'clock.
　　Tom: It's time for breakfast in Beijing.
　　Amy: And it's time for PE class in Sydney.

【参考答案】

一、1. B 2. A 3. A 4. A 5. B
二、1. A 2. C 3. C
三、1. A 2. B 3. A 4. A
四、1. F 2. T 3. F 4. F 5. F
五、1. C 2. A 3. A 4. C 5. B
六、1. A 2. A 3. A 4. B
七、1. C 2. B 3. A 4. A 5. C
八、1. B 2. D 3. A 4. C

九、任务一：1.—D 2.—C 3.—A 4.—B
　　任务二：1. dinner
　　　　　　2. It's time for breakfast
　　　　　　3. It's time for lunch

B Let's talk Let's play

一、1. C 2. C 3. B
二、1. A 2. C 3. A 4. A 5. C
三、1. six; dinner
　　2. ten; English
　　3. seven; breakfast
　　4. three; PE
　　5. four; computer
　　6. nine; music

B Let's learn Let's play

一、1. D 2. B 3. A 4. C
二、1. to 2. for 3. for 4. to
三、1. × 2. √ 3. √ 4. √

四、任务一：
　　第一行：go to school; go home; go to bed
　　第二行：6:30; 12:00
　　任务二：1. B 2. C
　　任务三：I have lunch at school at half past twelve.（答案不唯一）

B Read and write-Let's sing

一、4 3 2 1
二、任务一：1. ten o'clock; maths
　　　　　　2. six o'clock; get up
　　任务二：画图略
　　　　　　A: What time is it?
　　　　　　B: It's eleven o'clock. It's time for PE class.（答案不唯一）

听力材料及

Unit 1 My school

A. Let's talk   Look, ask and answer

一、1. C   2. C   3. A

二、1. A   2. B

三、1. F   2. T   3. T

四、1. on   2. second floor
   3. teachers' office   4. next to

A. Let's learn   Let's do

一、1. Where   2. first   3. two
   4. playground   5. library

二、1. C   2. A   3. B   4. D

三、1. B   2. D   3. C   4. A

四、B

A. Let's spell

[听力材料]

一、Jennifer is having dinner with her sister, Jane.

Jennifer says, "Let's eat all the vegetables. I will be better. I will be a shooter."

"Yes. But I will be a baker," Jane says.

[参考答案]

一、dinner; her; sister; better; shooter; baker

二、1. 圈出 driver 和 winter
   2. 圈出 dancer 和 computer
   3. 圈出 runner 和 swimmer

三、1. dinner   2. eraser; ruler

3. water; sister

Unit 1   阶段复习

[听力材料]

一、1. water   2. under   3. second
   4. library   5. teachers' office

二、1. Dinner is ready.
   2. No water near the computer.
   3. I read books in the library.
   4. This is my sister.
   5. The teachers' office is on the first floor.

三、1. Go to the library. Read a book.
   2. Go to the playground. Play football.
   3. Go to the garden. Water the flowers.
   4. Go to the teachers' office. Say hello.

四、听第一段对话，完成第1、2小题。

W：Welcome to our school!

M：How beautiful!

W：Thank you.

M：Is that your playground?

W：Yes, it is. And a beautiful garden is next to it.

听第二段对话，完成第3、4小题。

W：Excuse me. Where is the library?

M：It's on the second floor. It's next to Classroom 3.

W：Is the teachers' office on the second floor, too?

M：No, it isn't. It's on the first floor. It'

Salesperson: Sure. Here you are.

...

Salesperson: 5. _____

Lily: Yes. They are just right.

十、根据图片选择正确的答案,将其序号填入题前括号里。(10%)

(   ) 1. —What's the weather like? —It's _____.
　　　　A. sunny　　　　　B. rainy

(   ) 2. —Whose farm is this? —It's _____.
　　　　A. John's　　　　　B. Mike's

(   ) 3. —Are those horses? —_____
　　　　A. Yes, they are.　　B. No, they aren't.

(   ) 4. —Where is the girl? —She's on the _____.
　　　　A. first floor　　　　B. second floor

(   ) 5. —How much is the milk? —It's _____.
　　　　A. $1　　　　　　　B. ¥1

十一、阅读信件,判断下列句子正误,正确的写"T",错误的写"F"。(10%)

Grandma,

　　How are you? Thank you for your gift. I like the beautiful hat. I'm in Hangzhou now. It's sunny and hot today. I can wear the new hat. The food in Hangzhou is yummy but expensive. I like the noodles very much.

　　I miss(想念) you, Grandma. I miss your big farm too. The ducks are cute, and the sheep are fat. I love them so much. How are they now?

　　Please write back soon.

　　　　　　　　　　　　　　　　　　　　　　　Love,
　　　　　　　　　　　　　　　　　　　　　　　Peter

(   ) 1. It's rainy and hot in Hangzhou today.

(   ) 2. Peter has a new hat. It's beautiful.

(   ) 3. The food in Hangzhou is not expensive.

(   ) 4. Peter's grandma has some ducks and sheep.

(   ) 5. Peter has a big farm.

浙江省某市期末核心能力评价

评价范围：四年级下册

班级：_____ 姓名：_____

Listening Part(40%)

一、听录音，选择你所听到的内容，将其序号填入题前括号里。(8%)

(　)1. A. shoe　　　　　B. shirt　　　　　C. short
(　)2. A. cow　　　　　B. come　　　　　C. carrot
(　)3. A. 4:15　　　　　B. 5:15　　　　　C. 6:50
(　)4. A. first　　　　　B. four　　　　　C. forty
(　)5. A. wet　　　　　B. weather　　　　C. sweater
(　)6. A. this　　　　　B. these　　　　　C. those
(　)7. A. sunny　　　　B. snowy　　　　　C. rainy
(　)8. A. maths　　　　B. mouth　　　　　C. music

二、听对话，选择与你所听到的内容相符的图片，将其序号填入题前括号里。(12%)

三、听录音，选择正确的答语，将其序号填入题前括号里。(10%)

(　)1. A. They're shoes.　　B. They're pink.　　C. They're mine.
(　)2. A. It's nice.　　　　B. Yes, I like it.　　C. Yes, I do.

十、阅读语段，完成下列任务。(15%)

Hi, my name is Juby. I'm from the UK. I am in London. It's sunny today. It's 11:00 in the morning now. Time for brunch(早午餐). In the UK, we use forks and knives. I have fish and chips for my brunch.

Hello, I'm Andy. I'm from America. It's cool today. It's 8 a.m. in Seattle. Time to go to school. There are 20 students in my class. My classroom is on the second floor. It's next to the music room.

Hello, I am Qingqing. I am in Chongqing. It's 6:00 in the evening now. It's very hot here. It's time for dinner. We'd like to have hot pot for dinner. Welcome to my hometown(家乡).

任务一：根据语段内容判断下列句子正误，正确的写"T"，错误的写"F"。(10%)

(   )1. Juby lives in London, America.

(   )2. Juby has fish and chips for brunch.

(   )3. It's 8 a.m. in Seattle. It is cold.

(   )4. Andy's classroom is near the art room.

(   )5. Qingqing wants to have hot pot for dinner.

任务二：根据语段内容，补全下列句子。(5%)

1. In the UK, people use _____ and _____.

2. Andy's classroom is on the _____.

3. Qingqing's hometown is _____.

期末核心能力评价

评价范围：四年级下册

班级：_____ 姓名：_____

Listening Part (40%)

一、听录音，选择你所听到的句子中含有的单词或短语，将其序号填入题前括号里。(10%)

( ) 1. A. coat   B. skirt   C. shirt

( ) 2. A. dress   B. scarf   C. T-shirt

( ) 3. A. school   B. playground   C. garden

( ) 4. A. expensive   B. cheap   C. pretty

( ) 5. A. put on   B. wear   C. use

二、听录音，判断下列图片与你所听到的内容是否相符，相符的在括号里打"√"，不相符的打"×"。(10%)

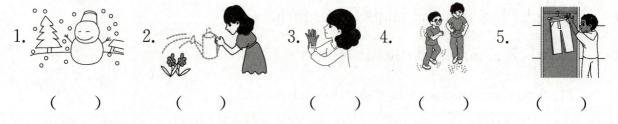

1. ( )   2. ( )   3. ( )   4. ( )   5. ( )

三、听录音，选择正确的答语，将其序号填入题前括号里。(10%)

( ) 1. A. It's forty-five.   B. They are forty-five yuan.
       C. It's forty-five yuan.

( ) 2. A. It's on the chair.   B. They are on the chair.
       C. It's green.

( ) 3. A. It's white.   B. It's a hat.   C. It's cloudy.

( ) 4. A. It's John's.   B. They're John's.   C. It's John.

( ) 5. A. Yes, it is.   B. It's on the first floor.
       C. Of course. Here you are.

Pingping: I like it. How much is it?

Shop assistant: Eighteen yuan.

Pingping: OK. I'll take it.

(　) (　) (　) (　) (　)

Total(总价): ￥_____

十一、任务型阅读。(12%)

1. I'm shopping for clothes.

I see a pretty skirt.

I try on the _____.

2. The skirt doesn't fit.

It is too _____.

I don't buy the skirt.

3. I see a pretty dress.

I try on the _____.

4. The dress doesn't fit.

It is too _____. I don't buy the dress.

5. I see a pretty coat.

I try on the coat.

It looks _____.

6. The coat fits.

I buy the _____.

任务一:根据图片选择合适的单词补全句子,将其序号填在横线上。(6%)

A. long B. coat C. nice D. skirt E. big F. dress

任务二:判断下列句子正误,正确的写"T",错误的写"F"。(6%)

(　)1. I'm shopping for fruit.

(　)2. The dress is too short for me.

(　)3. I buy the pretty coat.

核心能力评价（六）

评价范围：Unit 6

班级：_____ 姓名：_____

Listening Part(40%)

一、听录音，用数字给下列图片排序。(12%)

( )   ( )   ( )   ( )   ( )   ( )

二、听录音，写出下列物品的价格。(写阿拉伯数字)(8%)

1. ¥	2. ¥	3. ¥	4. ¥

三、听录音，选择正确的答语，将其序号填入题前括号里。(10%)

(   ) 1. A. They're thirty.　　B. It's thirty yuan.　　C. They are thirty yuan.

(   ) 2. A. Yes, it's nice.　　B. No. It's cheap.　　C. No. It's expensive.

(   ) 3. A. It's very pretty.　　B. It's ten yuan.　　C. They are very pretty.

(   ) 4. A. Yes, they are.　　B. Of course.　　C. No, it isn't.

(   ) 5. A. They're yellow.　　　　　　　　　　B. They are just right.

　　　　C. They're on the table.

四、听短文，填写所缺单词。(10%)

Look! Many clothes are on the sofa. The 1._____ are black. The 2._____ are nice. The 3._____ is blue. The 4._____ is white. It's 5._____. We like them very much.

居). They love red so much. Li Yuanyuan is wearing a red Chinese dress (qipao) and a red scarf. She is my best friend. Her little sister Li Jia is wearing a red sweater and a red hat. Zhang Xi, a tall and cool Chinese boy is wearing red pants. Haha...Look! Cat Mimi is wearing a red jacket, too. They say these are their clothes for the Chinese New Year.

Oh, there are some red lanterns outside my house. Do you like them?

Love,

Jessica

任务一:请在照片里圈出文中提到的三名中国小朋友,并与他们的名字连线。(6%)

任务二:根据短文内容,判断下列句子正误,正确的写"T",错误的写"F"。(8%)

(　　)1. Jessica enjoys her first Chinese New Year in China.

(　　)2. Chinese people love wearing red clothes during the Spring Festival.

(　　)3. Cat Mimi is wearing a red dress.

(　　)4. There are some red paper planes outside Jessica's house.

任务三:春节你穿什么样式的衣服呢?请仿照句子写一写。(5%)

Jessica: I wear a red Tang suit(唐装) at the Spring Festival.

_____

_____

核心能力评价(五)

评价范围:Unit 5

班级:_____ 姓名:_____

Listening Part(40%)

一、听录音,选择你所听到的内容,将其序号填入题前括号里。(10%)

( )1. A. shirt   B. T-shirt   C. skirt

( )2. A. socks   B. shoes   C. shorts

( )3. A. put on   B. put away   C. hang up

( )4. A. I like those shoes.   B. I like those pants.
       C. I like those socks.

( )5. A. Whose sweater is it?   B. Whose coat is it?
       C. Whose jacket is it?

二、听录音,选择与你所听到的内容相符的图片,将其序号填入题前括号里。(8%)

( )1. A.  B.   ( )2. A.  B.

( )3. A. 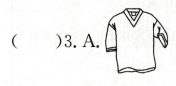 B. 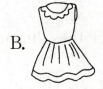   ( )4. A.   B.

三、听录音,选择正确的答语,将其序号填入题前括号里。(10%)

( )1. A. Brown.   B. Bikes.   C. Big.

( )2. A. It's purple.   B. It's 9:10.   C. It's a sweater.

( )3. A. They're my pants.   B. It's Kate's.   C. They're Kate's jeans.

( )4. A. They're under the chair.   B. They're orange shoes.
       C. They're my brother's.

十、根据图片顺序,用数字给下列句子排序,使其组成一篇完整的短文。(10%)

(　　)We help the farmer pick the tomatoes.

(　　)We are on a big farm today. We help the farmer feed the rabbits.

(　　)We help the farmer feed the hen.

(　　)We ride the horses on the farm.

(　　)We help the farmer milk the cow.

十一、任务型阅读。(14%)

　　Hi, I'm Jack. Welcome to my farm. My farm is so big. There are many animals on the farm. I have 15 cows, 20 sheep, 19 hens and 10 horses. And there are many vegetables. Look at the tomatoes, potatoes, onions and carrots. They are fresh(新鲜的). I like my farm very much.

任务一:在文中提到的动物和蔬菜下打"√"。(8%)

Animal					
Vegetable					

任务二:根据短文内容填空。(6%)

1. Jack's farm is very _____.

2. He has ten _____.

3. The vegetables are _____.

核心能力评价（四）

评价范围：Unit 4

班级：_____ 姓名：_____

Listening Part(40%)

听力音频

一、听录音,选择你所听到的单词,将其序号填入题前括号里。(12%)

(   )1. A. fork   B. for   (   )2. A. world   B. work

(   )3. A. potato   B. tomato   (   )4. A. cow   B. hen

(   )5. A. those   B. these   (   )6. A. sheep   B. horse

二、听录音,选择正确的答语,将其序号填入题前括号里。(8%)

(   )1. A. There are five.   B. They are lambs.   C. They are on the farm.

(   )2. A. There are two.   B. No, they aren't.   C. Yes, they are.

(   )3. A. They're orange.   B. They're red.   C. They're green.

(   )4. A. Yes, it is.   B. No, I don't.   C. Yes, they are.

三、听对话,选择同学们想要吃的食物,将其序号填在相应的方框里。(10%)

Mike □   Amy □   Sarah □   John □   Oliver □

A.   B.   C.   D.   E.

F.   G.   H.   I.   J.

四、听短文,判断下列句子正误,正确的写"T",错误的写"F"。(10%)

(   )1. Jack lives on a farm.

(   )2. There are not any horses on the farm.

(   )3. The sheep are running.

Sally: Let me see. 6. _____

A. What's the weather like there?	B. What time does the class begin?
C. It's sunny and hot.	D. We can have class in the gym.
E. It's rainy.	F. We can't go to the playground.

九、任务型阅读。(16%)

My Day

7:30 a.m.	9 a.m.	10 a.m.	12:00	3:15 p.m.

任务一：选择正确的答案，将其序号填入题前括号里。(10%)

(   )1. It's _____. It's sunny outside. I go to school.

　　　A. seven o'clock　　　B. seven thirty　　　C. seven forty

(   )2. It's 9 o'clock in the morning. It's time for _____.

　　　A. art class　　　B. computer class　　　C. Chinese class

(   )3. It's ten o'clock. I go to the _____. It's on the first floor.

　　　A. teachers' office　　　B. playground　　　C. library

(   )4. It's twelve o'clock. It's time for _____.

　　　A. breakfast　　　B. lunch　　　C. dinner

(   )5. I have a PE class at _____.

　　　A. 3:15 p.m.　　　B. 3:15 a.m.　　　C. 3 p.m.

任务二：根据表格内容和提示，用"It's time for..."或"It's time to..."完成下列句子。(6%)

1. It's 7:30. _____

2. It's 9:00. _____

3. It's 3:15. _____

阶段核心能力评价

评价范围：Unit 1—Unit 3

班级：_____ 姓名：_____

Listening Part(40%)

一、听录音,选择你所听到的内容,将其序号填入题前括号里。(10%)

( )1. A. war　　　　　　B. bird　　　　　　C. ball

( )2. A. car　　　　　　B. far　　　　　　　C. farm

( )3. A. playground　　　B. library　　　　　C. classroom

( )4. A. English class　　B. music class　　　C. art class

( )5. A. Can I go outside now?　　　B. Can I go home now?

　　　 C. Can I have some soup?

二、听录音,选择与你所听到的内容相符的图片,将其序号填入题前括号里。(12%)

( )1. A.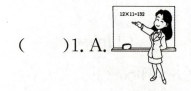B.　　( )2. A.B.

( )3. A.B.　　( )4. A.B.

( )5. A.B.　　　　　　　( )6. A.B.

三、听录音,选择正确的答语,将其序号填入题前括号里。(10%)

( )1. A. It's on the second floor.　　B. It's on the blackboard.

　　　 C. It's on the wall.

( )2. A. Yes, it is.　　　　　　　　B. Yes, we do.

　　　 C. Yes, we have.

2. —Is it snowy?

　—_____

　—_____

3. —_____

　—_____

　—Yes, it's windy.

十、任务型阅读。(14%)

Dear John,

　　How are you? I'm in Sydney now. It's sunny today! It's hot here. I can swim in the sea. Is it warm and sunny in Harbin? Can you play football?

Yours,
Mary

任务一:根据信件内容,选择正确的地点补全句子,将其序号填入题前括号里。(4%)

A. Sydney　　　　B. Harbin

(　　)1. John is in _____.　　(　　)2. Mary is in _____.

任务二:请根据图片提示帮助John完成回信。(10%)

Dear Mary,

　　I'm very sad. It is 1._____ and 2._____ −15℃ in Harbin. I can't go outside. And I can't 3._____ _____. I hope it will be 4._____ and 5._____ 20℃ soon.

　　Best wishes!

Yours,
John

核心能力评价（三）

评价范围：Unit 3

班级：_____ 姓名：_____

Listening Part(40%)

一、听录音,选择你所听到的句子中含有的短语,将其序号填入题前括号里。(10%)

(　　)1. A. cool and windy　　B. sunny and warm　　C. snowy and cold

(　　)2. A. sunny and hot　　B. rainy and cool　　C. cloudy and warm

(　　)3. A. in Sydney　　B. in London　　C. in Moscow

(　　)4. A. 26 degrees　　B. 35 degrees　　C. 13 degrees

(　　)5. A. have some soup　　B. have some water　　C. have some milk

二、听录音,判断下列图片与你所听到的内容是否相符,相符的在括号里打"√",不相符的打"×"。(10%)

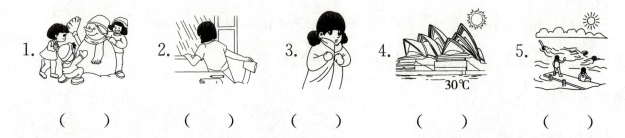

三、听录音,选择正确的答语,将其序号填入题前括号里。(10%)

(　　)1. A. Yes, it is.　　B. Yes, he is.　　C. Yes, I am.

(　　)2. A. It's here.　　B. It's on the first floor.

　　　　C. It's rainy now.

(　　)3. A. No, you can't.　　B. No, I can't.　　C. Yes, he can.

(　　)4. A. No. It's cool here.　　B. Yes, it's cool.　　C. Yes, it's cold.

(　　)5. A. No. It's cold here.　　B. I have a cold.　　C. Bless you!

2. Tom：What time is it in Cairo?

　　Amy：_____

3. Tom：What time is it in London?

　　Amy：_____

九、任务型阅读。(22%)

　　Hello, I'm Candy. I get up at six o'clock. I do morning exercises at six thirty. Then I go to school at seven thirty. I have four classes in the morning and two classes in the afternoon. After school, I play with my friend on the playground. Then I go home at four thirty. I do my homework at five o'clock. After dinner, I read books with my mother. Then I go to bed at nine o'clock.

任务一：根据短文内容，用数字给下列图片排序。(12%)

(　　)　　(　　)　　(　　)　　(　　)　　(　　)　　(　　)

任务二：阅读短文，判断下列句子正误，正确的在括号里写"T"，错误的写"F"。(10%)

(　　)1. Candy gets up at 7:00 and she goes to school at 8:00.

(　　)2. Candy has seven classes a day.

(　　)3. Candy goes to bed at 9 p.m.

(　　)4. It's three thirty. It's time for Candy to go home.

(　　)5. Candy reads books after dinner.

核心能力评价（二）

评价范围：Unit 2

班级：_____ 姓名：_____

Listening Part(40%)

听力音频

一、听录音,选择你所听到的单词或短语,将其序号填入题前括号里。(8%)

(　　)1. A. home　　　B. school　　　(　　)2. A. breakfast　　B. lunch

(　　)3. A. Chinese　　B. English　　 (　　)4. A. now　　　　B. new

(　　)5. A. thirty　　　B. thirteen　　 (　　)6. A. hamburger　B. number

(　　)7. A. go to bed　B. go to school　(　　)8. A. hurry up　　B. get up

二、听录音,选择与你所听到的内容相符的图片,将其序号填入题前括号里。(12%)

(　　)1. A.B.　　(　　)2. A.B.

(　　)3. A.B.　　(　　)4. A.B.

(　　)5. A.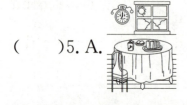B.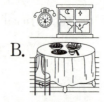　　(　　)6. A.B.

三、听录音,选择正确的答语,将其序号填入题前括号里。(10%)

(　　)1. A. She is from the UK.

　　　B. She is in the art room.

　　　C. She has breakfast.

Visitor: Wow! The lunch room is big and nice!

Sarah: Thank you.

八、连词成句。(9%)

1. playground   the   This   is   (.)

   _____

2. office   That   the   teachers'   is   (.)

   _____

3. that   school   your   Is   (?)

   _____

九、任务型阅读。(14%)

A. computer
B. school
C. classrooms
D. to
E. library

任务一：看图，选择合适的单词补全短文，将其序号填在横线上。(10%)

Welcome 1._____ our school. This is our classroom building(教学楼). We have two restrooms(卫生间) and two 2._____ on the first floor. We have a science lab(实验室), an art room and a 3._____ on the second floor. We have a teachers' office, a 4._____ room and a music room on the third floor. Our 5._____ is very big and nice.

任务二：根据图片补全下列句子，将答案写在横线上。(4%)

1. The music room is next to the _____.

2. The _____ is under the music room.

附录 II 核心能力评价（一）

评价范围：Unit 1

班级：_____ 姓名：_____

Listening Part（40%）

一、听录音,选择你所听到的单词,将其序号填入题前括号里。(10%)

( )1. A. four　　　　　B. floor　　　( )2. A. fourteen　　　B. forty
( )3. A. class　　　　　B. classroom　( )4. A. first　　　　B. second
( )5. A. playground　　B. library　　( )6. A. are　　　　　B. art
( )7. A. computer　　　B. music　　　( )8. A. garden　　　　B. gym
( )9. A. dinner　　　　B. sister　　 ( )10. A. river　　　 B. ruler

二、听录音,根据你所听到的句子的顺序用数字给下列房间排序。(12%)

三、听录音,选择正确的答语,将其序号填入题前括号里。(10%)

( )1. A. It's on the second floor.　　B. It's next to the teachers' office.
　　　 C. We have three teachers' offices.

( )2. A. Yes, it does.　　B. No, it isn't.　　C. Yes, I do.

( )3. A. Yes, it is.　　　B. We have a computer room.
　　　 C. No, we don't.

( )4. A. Forty students.　B. Four teachers.　C. This way, please.

( )5. A. Let's read a book.　　B. OK. We can play football there.
　　　 C. Let's water the flowers.

黄冈小状元作业本

知识清单

四年级英语下 RP

附录 I

知识清单

Unit 1 My school

▶ 语音知识

字母组合 er 在单词中的发音：

/ə(r)/: water 水 tiger 老虎 sister 姐妹 computer 电脑

▶ 重点词汇

Part A

first floor 一楼   second floor 二楼

teachers' office   library
教师办公室   图书馆

Part B

playground 操场   art room 美术教室

music room   computer room
音乐教室   计算机房

on the first floor 在一楼

next to 紧邻；在……近旁

read a book 看书

play football 踢足球

water the flowers 浇花

▶ 重点句型

常用单句

1. Excuse me. 打扰一下。

2. Here's my homework. 这是我的家庭作业。

1

3. Welcome to our school! 欢迎来到我们的学校！

4. This way, please. 这边请。

功能交际语

1. —Where's the teachers' office? 教师办公室在哪里？

   —It's on the second floor. 它在二楼。

2. —Is this the teachers' office? 这是教师办公室吗？

   —No, it isn't. The teachers' office is next to the library.

   不，不是。教师办公室挨着图书馆。

3. —Is that the computer room? 那是计算机房吗？

   —Yes, it is. 是的，它是。

4. —Do you have a library? 你们（学校）有图书馆吗？

   —Yes, we do. 是的，有。

5. —How many students are there in your class?

   你们班有多少名学生？

   —Forty-five students. 45名学生。

▶ 知识点拨

1. 询问某场所具体位置的句型及其答语。

   当你找不到某场所时，可以用"Where is…?"询问别人，意为"……在哪里？"。其答语为"It's in/on/next to…"。

   如：—Where is the zoo? 动物园在哪里？

   　　—It's next to the cinema. 它紧挨着电影院。

2. 确认某处是否为某场所的句型及其答语。

   一般疑问句"Is this/that…?"可以用来询问离说话人较近或较远的地点，意为"这/那是……吗？"。其答语为"Yes, it is."或"No, it isn't."

如：—Is this the art room? 这是美术教室吗？

—Yes, it is./No, it isn't. 是的，它是。/不，它不是。

3. 询问对方是否有某物的句型及其答语。

"Do you have...?"用来询问对方是否有某物，意为"你（们）有……吗？"。如果询问的物品名词为单数可数名词时，名词前要使用不定冠词a/an。其答语为"Yes, I/we do."或"No, I/we don't."。注意：答语要根据实际语境来选择用 I 还是 we。

如：—Do you have a storybook? 你有一本故事书吗？

—Yes, I do. 是的，我有。

—Do you have a canteen? 你们有餐厅吗？

—No, we don't. 不，我们没有。

▶ **文化视窗**

国外小学的课桌布置形式

国外小学的课桌布置有多种形式，目的是便于开展小组合作学习。下面介绍几种较为常见的形式。

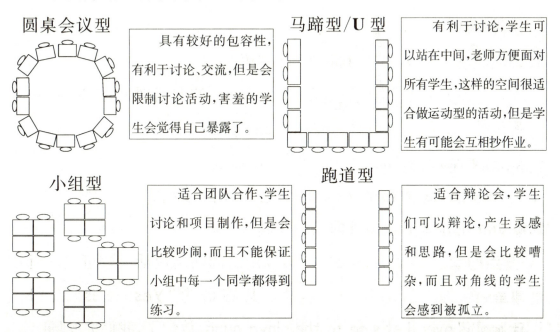

Unit 2 What time is it?

▶ **语音知识**

字母组合 ir/ur 在单词中的发音：

/ɜː/   girl 女孩   bird 鸟   nurse 护士   hamburger 汉堡包

▶ **重点词汇**

Part A

breakfast 早餐

lunch 午餐

dinner（中午或晚上吃的）正餐

English class 英语课

music class 音乐课

PE class 体育课

Part B

get up 起床

go to school 上学

go home 回家

go to bed 上床睡觉

jump and run 跳和跑

read and write 读和写

sing and dance 唱歌和跳舞

▶ **重点句型**

常用单句

1. School is over. Let's go to the playground. 放学了，我们去操场吧。

2. Time to go home, kids. 该回家了，孩子们。

3. It's time to get up. 该起床了。

4. Breakfast is ready. 早餐准备好了。

功能交际语

—What time is it? 几点了？

—It's 6 o'clock. It's time for dinner. 六点了。该吃晚饭了。

▶ 知识点拨

1. 询问时间的句型及其答语。

"What time is it?"常用来询问具体的时间，同义句为"What's the time?"。其答语为"It's＋时间."或直接回答时间。

如：—What time is it? 几点了？ —It's 9 o'clock. 九点了。

—What's the time? 几点了？ —Ten thirty. 十点半。

在英语中，时间通常有以下两种读法：

(1) 顺读法：钟点数＋分钟数

如：six fifteen(6:15) seven thirty(7:30)

eleven forty-five(11:45)

(2) 逆读法：分钟数＋past/to＋钟点数

①分钟数≤30分钟时，用"分钟数＋past＋钟点数"。

如：twenty past seven(7:20)

②分钟数＞30分钟时，用"分钟数＋to＋钟点数"。

如：twenty to eight(7:40)

另外，15分钟为"一刻钟"，在英语中可用"a quarter"表示；30分钟可用"half"表示。

如：a quarter past ten(10:15) a quarter to ten(9:45)

half past eight(8:30)

2. a.m. 和 p.m. 的正确使用。

(1)二者都不能单独使用,而要与表示时间的数字连用,且置于数字之后。

(2)不能与 in the morning 或 in the afternoon 连用,以免构成用词重复。

(3)不能与 o'clock 连用。

如:He gets up at 7 a.m. 他早上七点起床。

It's 5:30 p.m. now. 现在是下午五点半。

3. 表达"到了做某事的时间了"的句型。

"It's time for sth."意为"该做某事了"或"到了做某事的时间了"。它的同义句为"It's time to do sth.",在口语中常省略 It's。

如:It's time for school.＝It's time to go to school. 该上学了。

It's time for lunch.＝It's time to have lunch. 该吃午饭了。

▶ 文化视窗

Time Differences 时差

New York 19:00　London 00:00　Paris 01:00　Beijing 08:00

Tips:北京与伦敦的标准时差是 8 小时,即伦敦时间比北京时间晚 8 小时。英国在每年的三月底到十月底执行夏令时,那时的时差则为 7 小时。

Unit 3　Weather

语音知识

字母组合 ar/al 在单词中的发音：

ar/ɑ:/　arm 胳膊　car 小汽车　card 卡片

al/ɔ:/　tall 高的　ball 球　wall 墙壁

重点词汇

Part A

cold 寒冷的　cool 凉爽的

warm 暖和的　hot 热的

be careful 小心
go outside 去户外
weather report 天气预报

Part B

sunny 阳光充足的　windy 多风的

cloudy　　snowy　　rainy
多云的　　下雪的　　多雨的

hot and sunny 炎热且阳光充足的
cool and windy 凉爽且有风的
cold and snowy 寒冷且有雪的

重点句型

常用单句

1. It's cold outside. 外面冷。
2. It's 26 degrees. 是 26 度。

3. It's warm in Beijing today. 今天北京天气暖和。

4. Here's the world weather. 这里是世界天气预报。

功能交际语

1. —Can I go outside now? 现在我能出去吗？

   —Yes, you can./ No, you can't. 可以。/不行。

2. —What's the weather like in New York? 纽约的天气怎么样？

   —It's rainy. 是下雨天。

3. —Is it cold? 天冷吗？ —No, it isn't. 不，不冷。

▶ **知识点拨**

1. 询问自己能否做某事的句型及其答语。

   "Can I...?"用于询问他人的意见，意为"我能……吗？"。其答语为"Yes, you can. / Sure. / Certainly. / No, you can't."等。

   如：—Can I go to the park? 我能去公园吗？

   　　—Yes, you can. 可以。

2. 询问某地天气状况的句型及其答语。

   "What's the weather like in...?"用来询问某地的天气情况，意为"……天气怎么样？"。其答语为"It's sunny/windy/rainy/…"。

   如：—What's the weather like in Shenyang? 沈阳的天气怎么样？

   　　—It's cold and snowy. 天气寒冷又下雪。

3. 确认天气情况是否如此的句型及其答语。

   一般疑问句"Is it＋描述天气状况的形容词?"用来确认天气情况是否如此。其答语为"Yes, it is."或"No, it isn't."。

   如：—Is it cold? 天气冷吗？

   　　—Yes, it is. /No, it isn't. It's warm. 是的。/不冷，很暖和。

文化视窗

温度计量单位华氏度和摄氏度的区别

Tips:

华氏度＝32＋摄氏度×1.8 摄氏度＝(华氏度－32)÷1.8

(摄氏温标的单位为"℃",华氏温标的单位为"℉")

Unit 4　At the farm

语音知识

字母组合 or 在单词中的发音：

/ɔː/　horse 马　fork 叉子　/ɜː/　homework 家庭作业　world 世界

重点词汇

Part A

tomato
西红柿

potato
马铃薯；土豆

Part B

cow
母牛；奶牛

horse
马

carrot 胡萝卜　　　　green beans 豆角;四季豆　　　hen 母鸡　　　　sheep 羊;绵羊

these carrots 这些胡萝卜

a lot of animals 许多动物

over there 在那边

▶ **重点句型**

常用单句

You have a lot of animals! 你有很多动物!

功能交际语

1. —Are these carrots? 这些是胡萝卜吗?

   —Yes, they are. 是的。

2. —What are these? 这些是什么?

   —They're tomatoes. 它们是西红柿。

3. —What are those? 那些是什么?

   —They're horses. 它们是马。

4. —How many horses do you have? 你有多少匹马?

   —Seventeen. 十七匹。

5. —Are they hens? 它们是母鸡吗?

   —No, they aren't. They're ducks. 不,不是。它们是鸭子。

▶ **知识点拨**

1.询问近处或远处某些事物的名称的句型及其答语。

"What are these/those?"是用来询问某些事物是什么的句型,意为"这些/那些是什么?"。其答语为"They're＋事物名称(名词复数).".

如：—What are these? 这些是什么？

—They're hens. 它们是母鸡。

—What are those? 那些是什么？

—They're carrots. 它们是胡萝卜。

2. 确认近处或远处某些事物的名称的句型及其答语。

"Are they/these/those...?"是用来确认某些事物是否是什么的句型，其答语为"Yes, they are./No, they aren't."。

如：—Are these bananas? 这些是香蕉吗？

—Yes, they are./No, they aren't. 是的。/不，不是。

3. 询问对方所拥有的东西的数量的句型及其答语。

"How many...do you have?"是询问对方有多少东西的句型，其答语为"I have＋数字（＋可数名词单/复数）."或直接回答数字。

如：—How many dogs do you have? 你有多少只狗？

—I have three(dogs)./Three. 我有三只（狗）。/三只。

▶ 文化视窗

中西方文化中"鱼"的不同寓意

中西方文化有时对同一种动物赋予的含义不同。汉语中的"鱼"(fish)和"余"谐音，且"余"有富足之意，因此，"鱼"被认为是能给老百姓带来富裕生活的吉祥物。中国人在过春节时，除夕夜的餐桌上不能没有鱼。

在英语中，"鱼"常含有贬义色彩，一般用来形容不好的人或事，如"neither fish nor fowl"（不伦不类）、"cold fish"（态度冷淡的人）、"odd fish"（古怪的人）等。

Unit 5 My clothes

▶ **语音知识**

字母组合 le 在单词中的发音：

/l/ apple 苹果   people 人；人们   table 桌子

▶ **重点词汇**

Part A   **Part B**

hat （常指带檐的）帽子   skirt 女裙   coat 外衣；大衣   shirt （尤指男士）衬衫

pants 裤子   dress 连衣裙   jacket 夹克衫   shorts 短裤

clothes 衣服；服装   sock 短袜   sweater 毛衣

put on 穿；戴   hang up 挂起来   whose coat 谁的大衣
take off 脱掉   put away 收起来   pack my clothes 收拾我的衣服

▶ **重点句型**

常用单句

1. They're Chen Jie's. 它们是陈杰的。

2. I like that green skirt. 我喜欢那条绿色的短裙。

功能交际语

1. —Are these yours? 这（双鞋）是你的吗？
   —No, they aren't. 不，不是。

2. —Is this John's? 这是约翰的吗？
   —No, it isn't. It's Mike's. 不是。它是迈克的。

3. —Whose coat is this? 这是谁的外套？
   —It's mine. 它是我的。

4. —Whose pants are those? 那条裤子是谁的？
   —They are your father's. 它们是你爸爸的。

▶ **知识点拨**

1. 确认某物是否为某人的物品的句型及其答语。

   "Is this/that John's/…?"意为"这/那是约翰的/……吗？"，用于确认某单件物品是否为某人的，其答语为"Yes, it is./No, it isn't."。

   "Are these/those yours/…?"意为"这些/那些是你（们）的/……吗？"，用于确认多件物品是否为某人的，其答语为"Yes, they are./No, they aren't."。

   如：—Is this yours? 这是你的吗？ —No, it isn't. 不是。

   —Are those Mike's? 那些是迈克的吗？ —Yes, they are. 是的。

2. 询问物品归属的句型及其答语。

   "Whose＋单件物品＋is this/that?"意为"这/那是谁的……？"，其答语为"It's＋名词性物主代词/名词所有格."。

   "Whose＋多件物品＋are these/those?"意为"这些/那些是谁的……？"，其答语为"They're＋名词性物主代词/名词所有格."。

   如：—Whose dress is this? 这是谁的连衣裙？

   —It's Amy's. 它是埃米的。

   —Whose shoes are those? 那双鞋是谁的？

   —They are mine. 它们是我的。

文化视窗

Some Traditional Clothes 一些传统服饰

hanfu

kilt

kimono

sari

Unit 6 Shopping

语音知识

ar/ɑ:/ card 卡片   park 公园   er/ə(r)/ computer 计算机 dinner 晚餐

ir/ɜ:/ girl 女孩   sir 先生   ur/ɜ:/ turn 顺序   nurse 护士

al/ɔ:/ mall 购物中心 wall 墙壁   le/l/ little 小的   people 人;人们

or/ɜ:/ homework 家庭作业   work 工作   /ɔ:/ fork 叉子   horse 马

重点词汇

Part A | Part B

glove
（分手指的）手套

scarf
围巾

pretty
美观的；精致的

nice
好的

umbrella
雨伞

sunglasses
太阳镜

¥30
cheap
便宜的

¥120
expensive
昂贵的

Part A	Part B
try on 试穿　　put on 穿上 too small 太小　　too big 太大	a pretty dress 一条漂亮的裙子 how much 多少钱

▶ **重点句型**

常用单句

1. Let's try size 7. 我们试试 7 号吧。　2. They're just right. 它们正好。

3. It's very pretty. 它很漂亮。　　　4. It's too expensive. 它太贵了。

功能交际语

1. —Can I help you? 我可以帮您吗？/您需要买些什么？

   —Yes. These shoes are nice. 是的。这双鞋不错。

2. —Can I try them on? Size 6, please. 我能试试吗？请给我拿 6 号的。

   —Of course. Here you are. 当然可以。给您。

3. —Are they OK? 它们合适吗？

   —No. They're too small. 不合适。它们太小了。

4. —How do you like this skirt? 你觉得这条短裙怎么样？

   —It's very pretty. 它很漂亮。

5. —How much is this skirt? 这条短裙多少钱？

   —It's $89. 它 89 美元。

▶ **知识点拨**

1. "Can I help you?"的用法。

   "Can I help you?"意为"我可以帮您吗？"或"您需要买些什么？"，是商场、饭店等服务场所服务人员招呼顾客的用语，其答语为"Yes. I want/I'd like…"或直接回答想要的东西。

如：—Can I help you? 我可以帮您吗?

—Yes. I want a white shirt. 是的。我想要一件白色的衬衫。

2. 请求试穿/试戴某商品的句型及其答语。

"Can I try…on?"和"Can I try on…?"是用来提出可否试穿/试戴某商品的句型，意为"我可以试试……吗?"，其答语可以为"Of course./Sure./ …Here you are."。

如：—Can I try the shoes on? 我可以试试这双鞋吗?

—Of course. Here you are. 当然可以。给您。

3. 询问某商品价格的句型及其答语。

"How much is＋单个物品?"和"How much are＋多个物品?"是询问单个或多个物品价格的句型，意为"……多少钱?"，其答语为"It's/They're＋数字＋货币单位."或直接回答"数字＋货币单位."。

如：—How much is the pen? 这支钢笔多少钱?

—It's 18 yuan./18 yuan. 它18元。/18元。

▶ 文化视窗

服装的尺码

服装的尺码有两种常见标法。一种是 S（小）、M（中）、L（大）、XL（加大）等；另一种是身高加胸围的形式，如 160/80A、165/85A、170/85A。

在国家标准 GB/T 1335 中，女装上衣 S 号（小号）的号型是 155/80A；M 号（中号）为 160/84A；L 号（大号）为 165/88A。"号"指人体的身高，以厘米为单位表示，是设计和选购服装长短的依据；"型"指人的胸围或腰围，以厘米为单位表示，是设计和选购服装肥瘦的依据。如 165/88A，斜线前后的数字表示人体高度和人的胸围或腰围，后面的字母表示人的体型。人的体型分为 Y 体型、A 体型、B 体型和 C 体型。区别体型的方法是看胸围减去腰围的数值而定。